D0894787

The Desert Is Yours

The Desert Is Yours

by Erle Stanley Gardner

William Morrow & Company
New York 1963

Other Books of Travel and Adventure by Erle Stanley Gardner

THE LAND OF SHORTER SHADOWS
NEIGHBORHOOD FRONTIERS
HUNTING THE DESERT WHALE
HOVERING OVER BAJA
THE HIDDEN HEART OF BAJA

Published simultaneously in the Dominion of Canada by George J. McLeod Limited, Toronto. Printed in the United States of America by Connecticut Printers, Inc., Hartford. Library of Congress Catalog Card Number 63-20926.

Contents

List of Illustrations

The Desert Is Yours

Illustrations

The Desert Is Yours

Acknowledgment

It is difficult to extend individual credits for the photographs which accompany this book. Although Sam Hicks and I took most of the pictures, Jean Bethell took some of them and we called on J. W. Black for several of his color shots. Bob Boughton is an expert photographer, and so is John Straubel. They very courteously placed their pictures at our disposal, and we have used some of them. My friend Walt Wilhelm is an earnest and quite expert photographer, and a few of these shots were taken by him. In fact, it seems that all the people with whom I travel are "shutterbugs," and when we get home and compare photographs I pre-empt the better pictures. So I take this opportunity to extend my thanks to all the contributors.

Erle Stanley Gardner

Foreword

In this book I have tried to take the reader with me on a series of expeditions into little-known parts of the desert.

As we travel by airplane, helicopter, four-wheel drive automobile and Pak-Jak on a series of expeditions, the reader will be shown the old Emigrant Trail, will use a mine detector to unearth relics of the old covered wagon era, will soar into the air by helicopter to look for some of the famous lost mines, will fly over rugged mountain ranges, traversing ground in a few hours which has claimed the lives of many prospectors.

The reader will join a group of "rock hounds" in finding semiprecious gem stones. He will photograph old landmarks, go on daredevil, four-wheel-drive automobile trips.

In the end it is hoped he will know the desert as it is today, learn where he can go and what he can do if he takes the trouble to get the necessary equipment. He will meet some of the salty desert characters and will, I hope, feel refreshed by his experiences and learn to know and love the desert.

This book has no other objective than to take the reader on a series of adventures so that he can see for himself what the desert is like.

Erle Stanley Gardner

The Desert Is Yours

Chapter One
A Look at the Real Desert

From time immemorial the desert has been cast in the role of a sinister adversary.

Brooding in parched silence, the desert has been pictured as a furnace trap which lures its victims to their deaths. We hear stories of stranded motorists who, with sun-cracked skins and blackened tongues, stagger feebly to a highway and are rescued, or else fall in heat-induced delirium and leave their bleached bones for subsequent travelers to find.

There is an opposite side to this picture of the desert which I found when I first explored it years ago. In those days I would travel in my "camp wagon" out to some of its wildest parts. This second side of the desert story is one about which we hear too little—the health-giving side.

When I first knew the desert and came to love it, there were few roads that could be traversed with any degree of safety. Even the main roads were unsurfaced. Between Las Vegas and Barstow the road was a washboarded nightmare. Between Yuma and El Centro the road was a veritable gam-

Parts of the old plank road still remain.

ble with death. No matter what improvements were attempted on this stretch of roadway, the drifting sand would cover it. Then finally someone devised the idea of a plank road which would have no foundation at all, but would stretch like a winding ribbon, simply a line of rough boards tied together with metal strips. When the sand covered this road, workmen pulled the road on top of the sand. Then when the sand covered it again, the board road was once more raised above the sand.

During sandstorms this road was impassable. After the sandstorms it wound and twisted its sinuous way, first tilted dangerously to one side, then to the other, like a tortured snake.

It was not only a single-track road but its width was only a few inches more than the tread of the car. At long intervals there were turn-outs.

This road was very expensive to construct and maintain.

It was a jolting and hazardous experience to drive over it, but the desert dweller who had to use it, and who had been familiar with the old sand-covered road, considered it the last word in "conquering the desert."

Even in those days I found that the health-giving side of the desert, which was little publicized, was of great significance.

The majority of the people who dwelt there then told stories with a similar pattern. An individual who had been suffering with heart trouble, lung trouble, or some other disease that medical science had pronounced hopeless, had been given up to die by the doctors.

He had sought the solitude of the desert as a place where he could spend his last days as inexpensively as possible and without being a burden to friends and relatives.

Slowly but surely the gentle fingers of the desert had sought out the lesions and healed them. The tranquility of the desert silence, the freedom from tension, the pure, life-giving air accomplished wonders, and these unfortunate victims of civilization came to know the beneficent side of the desert, the caressing care of Mother Nature. They continued to live on and on.

To be sure, the desert is cruel. It has to be. The plant-studded surface where each individual growth seems to be cottony-soft in the sunlight is actually an optical illusion. Each plant is armed with myriad thorns, each thorn a needle-sharp bayonet. Sunlight glistens from these thorns to give an effect of great beauty—but don't dare brush even lightly against one of these innocent-appearing plants.

Those thorns not only are needle-sharp but they have microscopic barbs which make it very painful when one tries to extract them.

Extraction takes so much force the cactus spine may break off, leaving a good-sized thorn in the wound, and because of

At first glance the desert seems studded with soft and tufted plants . . .

. . . closer study shows that each tuft is a vicious, stiff spine . . .

these barbs it then becomes difficult for the body to eject the broken point by the usual process of having it fester out. Instead, after days of a painful sore, the thorn may become tolerated by the body, probably because the irritant coating (a type of natural desert creosote) will have dissolved. Then the thorn starts working its way deeper and deeper, the point will change direction because of muscular activity and then the person may find, to his surprise, a sharp, needle-pointed, almost transparent object emerging from his body many inches from the point of entry, long after the thorn entered the body.

In the span of a single lifetime I have seen great changes come to the desert; the Diesel engine, the caterpillar, the growth of transcontinental automobile traffic, the development of four-wheel-drive automobiles, the so-called dune buggies, the air-cooled two-wheel power scooters, the airplane, and, above all, the development of electric power and

. . . sharp as a needle and hard as a nail.

the construction of air-conditioned houses, have all contributed to changing the face of the desert.

The "civilization" which my friend the Chinese philosopher insists I must refer to only as "urbanization" marches relentlessly on. The desert can stop it in places, but the desert is continually retreating before it. During World War II General Patton wanted a place to train his tank troops where they could become accustomed to sand and terrific heat and learn to fight in an environment that would make the African desert seem familiar terrain to them when they arrived there with their tanks.

Artillery wanted a place to practice reasonably near centers of habitation, yet where they had virtually unlimited space for hurtling their death-dealing implements of warfare.

So the desert became a military training center, a dumping ground for artillery shells and air bombs.

Air conditioning revolutionized desert living in the settlements. The little village of Las Vegas became a huge sprawling city. Palm Springs started a gradual growth which suddenly mushroomed with the force of an explosion.

It became fashionable to spend weekends in the desert. Los Angeles, growing so that it was bursting its seams, had to have some nearby resort where people could get away from it all. Palm Springs was the answer.

From the viewpoint of the city dweller, the desert began to come into its own, but at the same time it began to melt away before the encroachments and "improvements" of urbanization and population pressures.

But the mystery of the desert and, in places, the danger of the desert remain unchanged. The desert can be spanned but it can't be conquered. It will co-operate with man in a health-giving program but it will never yield as the result of ruthless conquest.

Behind its façade of monotony, the desert is ever changing.

Sam Hicks, Jr. rides Pak-Jak to exposed mountain peak to get photograph demonstrating blast effect of wind-driven sand on solid granite.

Tom Farley, an old prospector of Sunflower Springs, showing off a weird rock.

The line of sand dunes always look the same, yet these sand dunes are marching and changing just like a line of surf at the seashore.

The rate of change in the sand dunes is, of course, slower but it is just as relentless.

During certain seasons of the year the desert is windy, and when the wind blows hard it carries particles of sand along with it. When something happens to slow the velocity of the wind, those sand particles are deposited.

Once a sand hill begins to form it slows the wind down so that more and more sand is deposited. The process is cumulative.

There are other changes, too.

Where the wind moves with great velocity, the sand particles carried on the wind are capable of cutting into solid granite boulders forming caves, pits and cracks.

For that reason the granite country in the desert is filled with wind-worn rocks of odd shapes.

Sometimes one finds old tent stakes which have been left in the desert—the bottom part, which has been protected by the dry soil, well preserved, the upper portions checkered by sunlight, worn by blowing sand.

Behind the solitude of vast open spaces is a certain eloquence.

At night when the winds spring up out of nowhere, the sand begins to drift and gradually makes the sound of a whisper, a peculiar, rustling whisper as it hits against the sides of cactus, Joshua trees, and prickly pear.

When the branches of the greasewood whip back and forth on the sand, they make a gentle, sibilant whisper.

Finally comes the most subtle whisper of all, the whisper of sand rustling against sand as it is borne on the wings of the night winds which will suddenly come up, blow for a while, then as suddenly die down.

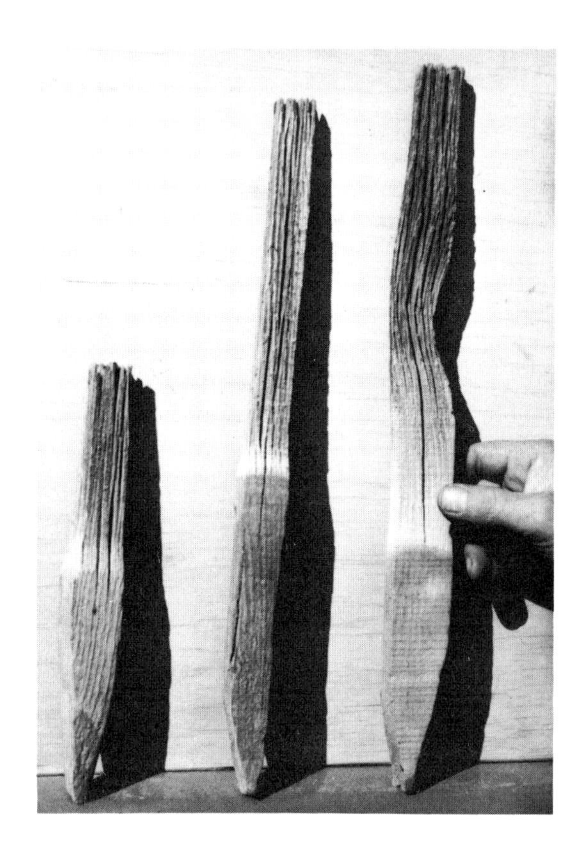

These ancient tent stakes were partially protected at the bottom by the ground, but blasted at the top by wind-driven sand.

Many times, lying in my sleeping bag and just dozing off, I have felt that those sand whispers made words, sometimes sentences. The sentences were soft and soothing and I would drift off to sleep with them in my ears. Then I would realize the sounds had been words and I would snap wide awake trying to remember what had been said. I would have the feeling that the whispering sands had given me some message that was important, but which I couldn't remember during my waking state any more than I could recall some vague dream.

Things that are left in the desert for any period of time show the mark of the desert.

Glass that lies in the shade of a bush will be etched by moving sands until it has an opaque finish. Left in the sun, it will frequently take on a purplish hue and sometimes becomes a deep lavender.

This change in color depends to a large extent on the

chemical composition of the glass, on the length of time that it has been exposed to the sunlight, and various other factors.

At rare intervals, the desert traveler may come upon a pile of discarded articles including a bottle that has not been broken. These lavender bottles are even greater treasures for the collector than the odd piece of glass.

The present generation knows little about the real mysteries of the desert: the stories of the lost mines, or the extent of the mineral wealth lying undiscovered in the region.

Anyone who has traveled fairly extensively in the desert can be certain that he has heedlessly passed over rich mineral deposits which would make him a wealthy man if his eyes could see only a short distance beneath the surface.

Now and then someone discovers a rich mine, but for the most part the easy-to-find discoveries have been located and exploited. The mineral that remains is, in most instances, beneath a surface that gives little clue to the location.

The desert could conceal a hundred lost mines.

It is exceedingly difficult for a man on foot to explore the desert mountain.

John Nummel, veteran prospector, tough as rawhide and wise in the ways of the desert, sat down in the shade of a paloverde tree to rest and take a few swallows of water from his canteen. His back was propped against a ledge of rock so ordinary that one would hardly give it a second glance. Yet from sheer force of habit the old prospector took his hammer and knocked off a piece of the weathered rock.

To his surprise, he found underneath the richest gold quartz he had ever seen.

He had no tools with which to develop a claim at the moment, and no provisions. Rather than stake out a claim that might be "jumped" during his absence, Nummel decided that since the gold had lain undiscovered for millions of years, a week or two more wouldn't make any difference. He carefully covered up his find and went down to take a job at the La Fortuna Mine below Yuma in order to get enough money to develop his claim.

The desert varies from place to place, but there is always the charm of open vistas.

He got the job, saved some money, tried to retrace his steps, and was never again able to find the gold ledge despite years spent in a fruitless search.

The desert is full of "lost" mines and there is a good reason why this is so.

There may be few landmarks in a given section of the desert. The country has a monotonous similarity of appearance yet is, paradoxically, subject to change. Cloudbursts in the hot summer months, winds that sweep up sandstorms, and the ever-drifting sand dunes, make the surface of the desert a place of shifting contours.

Somewhere up in the sand hills near Kelso, a teamster, driving a wagon laden with barrels of whiskey to satisfy the thirst of a mining community, found that one of the wheels on the wagon was giving way.

He drove the wagon far enough off the road where it would not present too great a temptation to some prospector who might stumble on it, took off the wheel, unharnessed the horses, lashed the wheel to the back of one of the horses and eventually reached town where he could secure the services of a blacksmith.

While the wheel was being repaired, a terrific windstorm came up and when the teamster rode his horses back to the place where he had left the wagon, he was unable to find it. The drifting sand had moved in, the wagon was buried, and to this day it has never been uncovered.

The true stories of the desert, fully vouched for, are almost incredible.

Within the last few days, while on a trip into the desert, I visited a man who was searching for a "lost" mine on a twenty-acre piece of property which he himself owned.

A tourist prowling around the place (and it is on a surfaced highway, one of the main arteries of the desert) broke off some rock from a ledge. The rock didn't look valuable but was unusually heavy. So the tourist took it along with him and eventually had it assayed. The rock ran something over twelve hundred dollars to the ton.

The man hurried back, tried to buy the twenty acres. Failing in that, because his eagerness aroused the owner's suspicions, he told the owner his story and suggested they open up the mine under an equitable financial relationship.

Then the tourist took the owner out to show him the ledge of gold-bearing rock. He couldn't find it.

This is only a twenty-acre plot. The man had carefully taken bearings from landmarks. He and the owner have repeatedly searched the property but so far they have been unable to find the place from which the tourist broke the rich ore. There are ledges all over the place. One of them is fabulously rich.

This is the story of the desert.

Today it is possible to get four-wheel-drive automobiles

We meet a typical dune buggy driven by Vern and Norm Reese of Paso Robles.

which can prowl into many isolated parts of it. The so-called dune buggies are made with large, low-pressure airplane tires which send the automobile fairly floating over the loose sand. The Pak-Jaks, the Burritos, the Tote Gotes, the Hondas, and dozens of other "scooters" furnish a means of transportation that will take the explorer far out into its trackless reaches.

It is easy if everything goes right. If anything goes wrong, the desert can still be the implacable, cruel enemy which took the lives of so many early pioneers and prospectors.

But for the most part things don't go wrong.

Yet even today, with all the new types of transportation available, only a comparatively few people realize the wonderful possibilities of the desert.

The desert is there. It is available. It furnishes excitement, health and recreation.

And the desert is yours.

Chapter Two
"Pinky" Takes Us Rock Hunting

Prospecting is one of the most fascinating activities known to man.

It has the thrill of hunting, the excitement of gambling, the element of possible danger, all rolled into one and spiced with a continuing suspense.

The next gully may contain a rich placer deposit. A man may be able to follow up a few "colors" to find where they come into the wash, then trace the trail of gold up to the side of a hill until he comes to a rich pocket worth many thousands of dollars.

Those peculiarly colored outcroppings up there on the side of the hill may indicate the presence of a really rich body of ore.

The game hunter, carrying his gun at the ready, stalks carefully through the forest knowing that at the next moment a deer may jump into view.

This knowledge gives the hunter a sense of constantly mounting excitement and suspense.

Hunting for gold in the desert has all this suspense, all

this excitement, and hunting for semiprecious stones is even better than hunting for gold because, while it is only rarely that one can hope to find a commercially profitable gold deposit, one can nearly always count on finding valuable semiprecious stones such as agates, jaspers, petrified palm, onyx and dozens of others.

Of course one has to know something about what to look for and where to look for it.

The geode, and its alter ego, the "thunder egg," have the most unprepossessing exteriors of any of the desert rocks. They look for all the world like common, ordinary round rocks the size of your fist, or perhaps half the size of your head. Almost any untrained searcher would pick up one and toss it disgustedly to one side, even after a reasonably close examination.

That unprepossessing exterior, however, masks a rock of unsurpassed beauty. The interior of the geode is an opales-

We invade an old mine in search of material which will polish.

cent substance, hard enough to take a fine polish. Sometimes it contains a hollow filled with colored crystals. Sometimes the interior is solid.

Sometimes this interior is of a uniform color, but more often it has graceful ribbons of opalescent loveliness.

The desert in prehistoric times was apparently well covered with palm trees, some of which are petrified and can be polished into magnificent cabochons.

Working in deposits of petrified palm wood, one occasionally comes across a piece of petrified palm root.

This is one of the hardest of rocks, almost as hard as a diamond, and when it is polished it shows a pattern of whorls and little independent concentric loops that make it not only a thing of beauty but also a splendid conversation piece.

Lavic jasper has the appearance of flint interspersed with a kaleidoscope of browns, reds and yellows. In some spots it can be picked up literally by the ton, and when properly

"Tumbled" rocks.

The tumbler is a huge steel drum in which rocks, with an abrasive, are sealed and polished.

polished and fashioned into bolo ties, cuff links, tie clasps, etc., it has a fascinating sheen with a delightful color pattern.

Apache tears, so-called, are round globules of obsidian which can be "tumbled" into handsome earrings and pendants.

In fact the desert is as a rule highly mineralized, and anyone who wants to subscribe to one of the "rock-hound" magazines can find plenty of places from which he can bring home all the semiprecious rocks he can possibly cut and polish.

The cutting and polishing is relatively simple.

There are dozens of firms making machinery which can be fitted into a corner of the garage and used to cut rocks into slices, shape the slices into cabochons, and polish them into highly individualized articles of jewelry.

Companies make a specialty of manufacturing settings into which these rocks can be placed; settings for earrings, brooches, cuff links, bolo ties, bill clips, etc.

It is also possible to "tumble" large quantities of rocks.

Perhaps the simplest tumbler is an old discarded truck tire. This empty casing can be placed on a wheel driven by a small electric motor so that it will revolve slowly.

The rock hound dumps a batch of semiprecious stones into the interior, puts in water and a grinding compound, then goes away and forgets the whole thing for a couple of weeks.

Then he comes back, washes off the rocks, puts them into another casing containing a very fine polishing compound and again forgets the whole thing for four or five days.

When he returns and washes off his rocks, he finds that he can fill a huge fish bowl with smoothly polished rocks which are a delight to the eye, and many of which can be used for jewelry without further cutting or polishing.

While the truck-casing method of tumbling rocks is the simplest and cheapest, there are now many commercial

Charles Remick makes a living in the desert, finding semiprecious rocks and selling them to rock hounds.

These rock hunters are philosophical in their outlook. Left to right: Paul and Doris Cogley, Mrs. Charles (Edith) King, Helen Ellison, Mrs. Claude Potter.

"tumblers" on the market. These are enclosed receptacles in which the rocks and abrasive material can be dumped and then are turned slowly by an electric motor. They turn out a finished product in a shorter time than by the use of the homemade tumbler with the truck casing.

In fact the fascination of "rock hounding" is more than a hobby. It is a passion. Once it gets into your blood it can become a dominating force.

And it is one of the most healthful of all hobbies.

There are of course dealers in semiprecious stones who make it a business to bring back from the desert large quantities of rocks which they sell in various "rock shops" throughout the country.

The average rock hound, however, uses what he finds, trades his surplus to other rock hounds and in the course of time makes up many articles which are kept on exhibit, worn proudly or given to friends.

Nor is rock hounding restricted to the young. In fact the rock hound often has passed the age of retirement and is searching for some healthful hobby.

Doris Bryant of Hemet, California, is outstanding as a rock hound, yet one could hardly call her typical. She has the individuality which is related to genius.

She is in her early sixties, small of frame, spare of flesh, and has the spirit of a championship prize fighter. She wants to live life her way and she resents regimentation or unnecessary restrictions.

It is essentially her freedom-loving nature which has brought her into such close contact with the desert.

When a person is out in the desert he is pretty much on his own, and Doris loves to be on her own.

Because she is too slight to ride Pak-Jaks, Burritos, Tote Gotes or other motor scooters, she goes in for pint-sized power vehicles that can be loaded in a pickup or on a trailer and then, once in the desert, will go just about anywhere.

When I first knew her she had a contraption that was in the nature of a miniature caterpillar tractor, only the treads were of rubber.

This vehicle was her pride and joy until she became acquainted with the Terra Gator.

The Terra Gator is a short, chunky vehicle reminding one somewhat of an overgrown bathtub, but it has six wheels with balloon tires, watertight construction, and it will go through mud, over sand and up such steep grades that it would seem to be in imminent danger of tipping over backwards.

Doris loves it.

She loads it either on a little trailer or, using an inclined ramp, drives it up to the bed of a four-wheel-drive pickup; then she starts out in the desert. When she gets to a likely-looking spot that she wants to prospect, she runs the machine

Doris Bryant at the controls of her Terra Gator.

Doris takes Pinky Brier on a quick run.

down the ramp, starts exploring the ground, and has the time of her life.

Doris has visited my ranch on occasion, bringing her various vehicles for demonstration and testing, and because I knew she was a prominent member of a rock-hunting club, I asked her about it.

The result was an invitation to visit her club when it was somewhere in the field.

Opportunity didn't present itself until February of 1963 when I had a couple of days free to explore, but I had quite a bit of country to cover and the question was how to get to where we were going.

The answer was "Pinky" Brier.

Pinky is an unforgettable character and a "flying fool."

Pinky took up flying thirty years ago. Her husband Joe Brier, was her instructor and he really did a job of teaching

Pinky insists that I take a ride.

Pinky is most definitely a character.

her to fly. He taught her just about everything there was to know.

Now she and her husband have a charter flying service called Tri-City Airport near San Bernardino. Joe, who is a marvel with engines, keeps the planes running with the precision and accuracy of a Swiss watch.

Pinky has the honor of being the first woman ever to be licensed as an instructor, and she has ferried wartime planes across the Atlantic, trained stunt flyers, and done just about everything any person could do in the air.

The training of stunt flyers was not just grandstanding. Pinky was one of the teachers who put them through their final acrobatics ("aeriobatics" is Pinky's word for it) in connection with combat flying, and when, as sometimes happened, she found herself assigned to an aviator who was inclined to feel a little superior and to adopt an attitude that

While Pinky and I are planning the route . . .

. . . we catch Sam taking a picture . . .

. . . then return to our planning.

Early morning shadows show the rough contours of the country.

no woman could teach *him* anything, Pinky would start a series of acrobatic gyrations that would cause the patronizing student to quit smiling, turn slightly green, become afflicted with acute nausea and, ultimately, after parting with all his breakfast and some of last night's dinner, to look at her with awe and respect. Then Pinky would go on with the instruction in a more orthodox manner.

Since I use Tri-City Airport a lot, we're destined to spend quite a bit of time with Pinky in this book as we go out on our various explorations in the desert, and I hope you will get to know her as I do. She is a genius at flying, an outstanding character and, thanks to her husband, always piloting planes that are kept up to the minute.

On this particular occasion, Pinky was to fly us out to the place where the rock hounds were camped and "buzz" the camp, then lead the way to an abandoned military flying field where the rock hounds would pick us up with automobiles and take us out to camp.

Because weather forecasts showed that my ranch at Temecula, with its nearby flying field, would be socked in, Sam Hicks and I drove over to Palm Springs and had Pinky pick us up there shortly after dawn.

That is one thing about Pinky: if she says she'll have a plane for you at a certain place at a certain time, that plane will be there. As a rule she won't be early because she has so many flying commitments, but unless there is some major emergency such as an unforeseen development in the weather, Pinky will never be late. On one occasion I had her fly six hundred miles to pick me up so she could then fly me back to my ranch at Temecula. Pinky said she would be there at eight o'clock in the morning.

Some friends came down to see me off. They pointed out that no woman could possibly fly six hundred miles before breakfast, that no woman could get up early enough to fly six hundred miles by eight o'clock.

They kept looking at their watches to prove their point.

At five minutes to eight they were smiling at each other; at three minutes to eight they were smugly nodding; at two minutes to eight they heard the sound of twin motors and turned to look.

At exactly ten seconds before eight o'clock Pinky taxied up to the ramp where my baggage had been placed and was out on the step of the plane. Jumping lightly to the ground, she accepted introductions with her customary poise, then with the help of Sam Hicks, my ranch manager and right hand on all our expeditions, she helped load the paraphernalia in the baggage compartment of the plane.

At exactly five minutes past eight, Pinky, Jean Bethell, my executive secretary, Sam Hicks and I were taxiing down the field and a minute or two later swept over my awe-struck friends with a roar as we started our six-hundred-mile journey back to my ranch.

Long, barren ridges could conceal many mines.

On another occasion, when conflicting dates made it seem that I would be forced to cancel a speaking engagement, something I was very reluctant to do as I had never yet canceled a speaking date in my life, I appealed to Pinky.

Could she pick me up at my ranch in Southern California, fly me to Boise, Idaho, in time to make a speech at an evening banquet and have me back at my ranch at eight o'clock the next morning to take part in a conference with a New York editor who was himself traveling on a split-second schedule?

Pinky said it not only could be done, but that she would do it.

And she did.

Because of Pinky's skill as a flyer, her enviable safety record and the condition in which she keeps her planes, her services are much in demand.

Four people can charter her plane in the evening, fly over to Las Vegas, spend an evening of pleasure watching the shows and testing their luck at the various games of chance, then have Pinky fly them back around one or two o'clock in the morning and the total transportation charge will be very little more than if they had decided to go by automobile.

As a result, Pinky spends a great deal of her time flying back and forth to Las Vegas, and actually keeps a car in Las Vegas as well as a place where she can stretch out and sleep while her passengers are seeing the sights.

Computing statistics on Pinky, one knows that she can't be a "spring chicken," but seeing her in the flesh one can hardly believe that she didn't take up flying when she was two years old, because she gives the impression of being well on the underside of thirty-five.

Pinky can jump from the wing of the plane to the ground as lightly as a bird. She can be as vivacious as a teen-ager and yet she has the poise of a diplomat.

I love the desert but I am a curious cuss and I want to

The Turtle Mountains from the plane.

Above a thin layer of soil rise barren peaks of sheer rock.

The mud volcanoes at the end of the Salton Sea.

know what it looks like from all sides. Before I go into a place I study what maps are available and then I invariably take a look at it from the air, taking a series of pictures which I develop and study with a magnifying glass. Then when I go into the country on foot or by Pak-Jak I have a pretty good idea of the topography. Later on, in case I arrange for helicopters to make a low altitude survey, I know exactly where I want to go and the points that I want to look at.

On the morning we were to meet at Palm Springs, Pinky was actually five minutes early.

Sam Hicks and I climbed in the plane, fastened the seat belts, Pinky gave a wave of her hand and we were on our way, climbing into the crystal-clear air of the desert.

I love exploring the desert in a chartered twin-motored airplane. If I had unlimited time and money I think I would spend almost every waking moment in desert exploration, either from the air or on the ground.

When one knows some of the legends of the desert, some

Hot, boiling mud pots.

of the stories of the famous lost mines, it is fascinating to fly over the terrain, correlate the various clues, and pick out the old well-traveled roads as well as the new ones. Also, when one is looking for fresh places to explore where there are no roads, an aerial reconnaissance at a reasonably low altitude is almost a necessity.

Pinky pointed out the line of the San Andreas fault, the famous fault which stretches the length of California and has been responsible for so many of California's devastating earthquakes.

Because water can find its way to the surface from this fault, when one gets in the desert the line of it is marked by a whole series of native palm trees strung out across the sand valleys. Some of these palm groves are located where they can be reached by four-wheel-drive automobile. Some places are so isolated that they are virtually exempt from discovery except from the air.

Leaving the line of the San Andreas fault, we swung off

Typical desert scenery.

to the east of the Salton Sea and cut across the Chocolate Mountains.

The sun was still low in the east, the shadows were long and black, the desert peaks were etched with golden brilliance.

Down below us somewhere, over a hundred years ago, Peg-Leg Smith had trudged along on his fateful journey—a journey that was destined to start one of the most fabulous of all the lost mine legends, and which in the course of time would cost the lives of many ambitious searchers.

The Lost Peg-Leg Mine and the Lost Dutchman Mine are probably the two most famous of all the "lost" mines, and may well be the richest.

Certain it is that they have led many a prospector to his death.

It is difficult to know how many people have perished in

the search for the Lost Peg-Leg Mine, but it is possible to get much better records on the Lost Dutchman Mine.

By those who know, something like three hundred and fifty persons to date have been estimated to have perished in the Superstition Mountains, their deaths caused directly and indirectly by searching for the Lost Dutchman Mine.

Even today one of the modern hostelries, complete with air conditioning, bar and restaurant and probably within less than twenty miles of the fabulous riches of the Lost Dutchman Mine, gives its guests this printed warning:

Do not go searching without adequate armed protection and guides. No handful of shining nuggets is worth a human life and strange disaster has stalked many in this awesome mountain.

And that is perhaps the understatement of the week.

Strange disaster indeed. The mystery surrounding the

Locale of Lost Dutchman Mine.

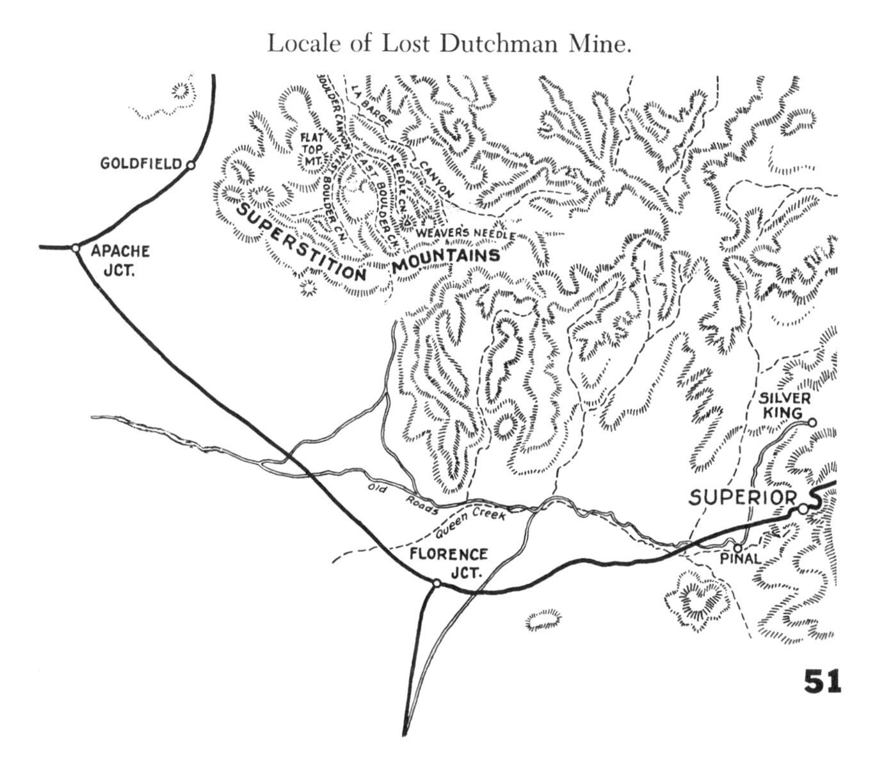

We fly over the desert . . .

deaths of those who searched for the Lost Dutchman Mine is far greater than the mystery of the mine itself.

Why have so many of these searchers been found with their heads literally severed from their bodies? And why is it that these people were almost invariably the ones who could have been counted on to rediscover the mine or perhaps may have done so?

There was quite a bit of speculation about these puzzling questions as we crossed the Chocolate Mountains, doubled back to pass over the Orocopia Mountains, the Chuckwalla Mountains, and then started following a road that Doris had outlined on our map.

For the first few miles the road was surfaced. Following Doris' instructions, we left the surfaced road and flew over a dirt road, then took several turns from the dirt road until we picked up distinctive landmarks, at which point we were supposed to be able to see the camp of the rock club.

. . . and come to the camp of the Rock-a-Teers.

With the aid of Sam Hicks' eagle eye it wasn't long before we spied the campers. Pinky put the plane in a descending spiral, buzzed the camp, and then took off on an air line for the abandoned military landing field that she knew of.

It took the rock hounds some time to locate a route to this field from the ground, but after exploring awhile they found one and came to meet us. Doris Bryant was in her jeep pickup, and Potter, the president of the club, in his jeep.

Pinky, Sam and I piled in the cars, carrying our battery of cameras, and made the relatively slow journey to the rock hunters' camp, a journey which took us almost as long via automobile as it had taken us to fly all the way from Palm Springs by air.

This particular group is called the Rock-a-Teers Mineral Society. It has strict bylaws.

It is a rule of the club that no man-made substance is ever left on the desert.

Pinky is interested in a specimen of twisted desert wood.

The author, far left, poses for a picture by Doris, holding camera at extreme right.

They don't bury their cans because they know from experience that coyotes are inclined to dig them up and leave them littered over the desert. With can openers they remove both ends of the cans, then they flatten out the cylinder so that all that is left of the can is three pieces of flat tin. These pieces are collected in sacks and taken back to be disposed of at regular municipal dumping grounds.

Not only do these people pick up their own litter but when they are in the desert they spend considerable time picking up litter left by others.

Seen from the air, their camp was beautiful. A group of house trailers, "campers" and four-wheel drive pickups were parked in the rough circle.

Seen at close range the camp was even more appealing; but its charm was primarily due to the people.

Many of the group are well past retirement age. They love the outdoors and the desert and have learned the lessons

The Rock-a-Teers gather around the author. Left to right: Paul and Doris Cogley, Clara Guy (sitting), Helen Ellison, Mrs. Glunt (Mrs. Potter's mother), Claude Potter, Dell Guy, the author (in front of Mr. Guy), Edith King, Charlie King.

of life. They know that the fruits of keen competition are not the most satisfying of life's rewards; that a life of live and let-live, of quiet friendship, companionship and philosophical relaxation offers far more lasting benefits than the dog-eat-dog school of existence.

For this reason there was a lack of tension in the camp. The people were there to relax, to enjoy the desert, to appreciate the beauties of nature, to pick up surface rocks, and, by the labor of cutting and polishing, transform them into things of beauty.

That camp somehow gave one the impression of being attuned to nature and to the spirit of the desert. Visiting this camp was as comfortable and soothing to the spirit as an old shoe is to a cramped foot.

The Rock-a-Teers were engaged in collecting a semi-precious stone, which, as it happened, had been discovered by Doris Bryant and apparently was new to gem hunters and rock hounds.

Onda Potter hammers off a specimen of the new type of semiprecious rock discovered by Doris Bryant.

Doris and her philosophical dog.

Samples of Doris' discovery cut and polished.

They were collecting chunks of rocks while we were there. Many of the Rock-a-Teers had with them pieces of this material which had been previously gathered, cut and polished. It was beautiful. They told us it was a new mineral combination and that they were going to try to have it named after Doris.

Of course, the collecting of rocks is in a way a secondary activity. It furnishes a springboard from which these people can launch their excursions into the desert. It gives them an excuse to get out and sit around the campfire at night, relaxed in a warm, cozy atmosphere, enjoying to the full the out-of-doors and the spirit of group companionship.

We walked around the camp and found not so much as a cigarette stub on the ground. These people are fanatics about leaving a "clean camp."

There were some touches of humor in connection with the camping experiences of these rock hounds. Doris, for

Doris hurdles a ditch . . .

. . . then scares me to death roaring up a steep slope.

instance, had once apparently lost her little Terra Gator when she was out in the desert, or became separated from it so that she had some difficulty finding it.

So now Doris carries a bright red flag on a long bamboo pole and whenever she leaves the Terra Gator to go exploring she puts the flag in place so it can be seen high above the tops of the desert brush.

When one realizes that the Rock-a-Teers is just one small club from one small California city and that almost every day various rock-hound clubs head their four-wheel-drive vehicles out into the desert to sample the seemingly endless supply of its natural resources, one can readily understand the importance of this activity. Economically rock hounds account for a lot of profitable business to the merchants in the cities where they live. In the camp of the Rock-a-Teers alone there were cars, pickups, trailers and various camp gadgets amounting to many thousands of dollars, all spent on this satisfying hobby.

I know from personal experience how great is the sense of satisfaction, that comes from picking up a seemingly ordinary rock in the desert, then cutting, shaping and polishing that rock until finally one has an object as artistic as a painting on canvas, and one every bit as highly personalized.

Very few rock hounds sell any of the things they make. They prefer to give their rock jewelry to their friends, or keep them for their collections.

The rock hunters are a relatively new development in the field of desert travel. The scooters, the four-wheel-drive vehicles, the big balloon tires, have given them an opportunity to penetrate parts of the desert which had hitherto been unexplored. They have discovered, in the aggregate, vast deposits of agate, jasper, etc., which have been made into beautiful articles for personal adornment.

More power to them.

Chapter Three
Plans to Explore Untrodden Areas

Probably no section of our country is richer in historical legends than the desert of the Southwest. These legends are hidden behind a façade of inscrutable mystery marked by weird monotony.

The casual traveler sees the face of the desert stretching endlessly, mile after mile, with eye-aching repetition.

Unless he ventures from the highways into an exploration of the desert mountains, or grinds his way down the long valleys in a four-wheel-drive automobile, he is inclined to think of the desert in the words of the traveler who said, "Here we have huge quantities of nothing."

But this seemingly repetitious scenery is one of the reasons that the desert has so many legends, such as the Lost Dutch Oven Mine.

Thomas Schoefield, the engineer working for the Santa Fe Railroad when the tunnel was being drilled from the Clipper Mountains to Danby, discovered a fabulously rich mine while prospecting on his day off. He returned to camp hysterical with excitement, his pockets loaded with gold—

Now passengers relax in air-conditioned trains as they ride smoothly over the desert.

yet he was never able to return to the scene of his discovery.

When we moved into this country with four-wheel-drive automobiles, Pak-Jaks and helicopters in an attempt to retrace Schoefield's footsteps, the reason for his confusion was readily apparent.

Today the desert is one of the most accessible of all adventure grounds in the world. People living in California, Arizona, New Mexico, Nevada, Utah have only to get in their automobiles, drive off, and within a few hours be in a land that is steeped in mystery and rich in legend.

Those in more distant parts of the United States can, within four or five days, drive over excellent paved roads to the land of adventure; or they can step aboard the luxurious Super Chief, go to Danby, and in this isolated desert community be within twelve miles of the site of the fabulous riches discovered and lost by Schoefield. The traveler will have glided smoothly over a perfect roadbed in air-condi-

There is geologic evidence of tremendous upheavals in the desert.

tioned comfort to within a few miles of a place which a hundred years ago could only be reached by someone with the physical stamina necessary to endure terrific hardship.

A person can step aboard a jet plane, fly to Phoenix, Arizona, rent a car and drive within an hour to a fine motel at Apache Junction. He can sleep in air-conditioned comfort, knowing that he is within less than twenty miles of the fabulous riches of the Lost Dutchman Mine. In the meantime he can be in one of the most healthful climates in the world.

Nor is the desert climate at all consistent, except during the summer months when the furnace heat causes the horizons to dance in mirage-distortion. Even in the first part of February, as we were gathering material for this book and planning to meet helicopters in the desert, the temperature in the deep shade at Amboy at four o'clock in the afternoon was an even hundred and four degrees. In the summer the intense heat can crack rocks, and the geological structure of the desert shows at times a crazy-quilt pattern.

The desert tortoise, however, with his well-camouflaged shell which even includes a built-in chin rest, takes the climate in his stride.

The desert is a land of startling contrast. At the same time, it is difficult to define where it begins and where it ends.

Land in the San Fernando Valley, which is now within the city limits of Los Angeles and presently valued by the front foot, was a sandy waste fifty years ago. Then came water from the aqueduct, and the land blossomed into small ranches of remarkable fertility. The ranches were subdivided into one-acre lots, and then, in turn, into building lots. Little shopping centers sprang up, merged together, and now this area is a mass of dwellings stretching back from main avenues composed of business properties.

Palm Springs is proud of the fact that it is desert, yet Palm Springs is rapidly becoming a community of swimming pools, golf courses, beautiful houses and stores that rival big city emporiums.

Forty odd years ago when I first knew Phoenix, it was a small city with the barren desert waiting just outside the paved streets. Now it is a great sprawling city covering many square miles and surrounded with resorts, ranches and fertile fields which intersperse the suburbs. From Phoenix to Mesa is virtually one sea of dwellings. Not until the tide reaches the base of the Superstition Mountains is there any end to urbanization, and then it stops abruptly.

The desert is for the most part fertile soil parched by lack of rainfall. High mountain ranges shut off the rain-bearing clouds and the only things that can grow are the plants designed by nature to conserve water and endure the blistering heat of the summer sun.

Unless we stop to think about it, it is difficult to realize

Fierce desert heat can cook eggs and crack rocks.

The desert tortoise has an elaborate camouflage.

the far-reaching functions of moisture, not only on the ground but in the air.

Where there is water, the sun evaporates it and the moisture-laden air thereupon forms a protective covering which cuts down the high actinic content of the sun's rays. In the desert, where there is no such protective covering because there is no water to evaporate, the fiery rays of the sun beat down with fury.

The plants that grow in the desert are for the most part protected by thorns so that hungry animals will not eat them, and with a coating of a natural creosote so that whatever moisture exists within the plant cells is sealed in and protected from evaporation.

In the desert there are no soft shadows and mellow sunlight such as exist where there is moisture in the air to diffuse the rays of the sun. In the true desert the shadows are so deep they appear black, and the sunlight so vivid it dazzles the eyes.

Human beings who would live in the desert must make either a natural or an artificial adjustment.

Dark glasses can keep the glare of the sunlight from burning the retina of the eye, can give the weary eye an opportunity to rest the muscles which would otherwise keep the pupils constantly contracted to pinpoints.

The typical desert dweller has gray or light blue eyes, and the muscles that control the pupils have been so developed that the pupils can remain as pinpoints without undue fatigue.

When I was new to the desert country, and before I realized what was happening physiologically, I wondered why I felt such gratifying relief on entering an adobe house where the walls were thick, the windows small, and the atmosphere one of cool tranquility. It was only after many such experiences that I began to realize that the muscles controlling the pupils of my eyes had become so completely weary in the glare of the sunlight that restful shade provided enormous relief. Apparently there is no sensation of acute pain in connection with ocular muscular fatigue of this type, and it is only when the muscles relax that one realizes how uncomfortable he has been.

The same is true of the glands that regulate perspiration.

I remember one time in Manila when I had been moving altogether too rapidly over a period of several days, trying to accomplish too much in too short a time. I was on the verge of total collapse. It wasn't until I boarded an outgoing steamer and stopped perspiring that I felt a most blessed sense of relief, followed by extreme drowsiness and relaxation. The body was so depleted of necessary chemicals from excess perspiration that my whole system was out of balance.

Man's body is an air-conditioned unit. Men can live in temperatures running from a hundred and twenty to a hundred and twenty-five or a hundred and thirty in the shade because they can perspire. As the perspiration evaporates, the skin is cooled so that the body temperature doesn't reach fever point.

However, the desert dweller uses little water and hardly *seems* to perspire.

Actually desert perspiration is deceptive. I have spent hot days in the desert when it seemed that I was perspiring little, if at all. My skin would seem to be dry. Actually I was perspiring a lot but the hot, dry air was evaporating the perspiration as soon as it came to the surface. My undergarments were dry but harsh with the salt left from evaporation, and where my clothes came in contact with a cushion which prevented the air from getting to my body, the fabric was soaking wet.

The main point, however, is that despite its drawbacks

The tragedy of greed. This mouse crawled through the opening of a syrup jug, gorged itself on syrup, and became too fat to escape.

and physical discomforts the desert still remains a place of adventure, a paradise of space, a land of beckoning enchantment.

As I mentioned earlier, it can also be cruel. But cruelty can be kindness, just as kindness can be the the most refined cruelty.

We see the latter type of cruelty in the overmothered child who has been indulged and spoiled to such a degree that later on, in making an adjustment to the realities of worldly existence, the grown-up individual is bound to undergo suffering, ostracism and bitter disappointment.

In the desert we see cruelty as kindness. The man who has been trained in the desert and by the desert is self-sufficient, competent, keen in his perceptions, quiet in his mannerisms and able to win and hold friends almost anywhere. Because any mistake can be fatal, the desert dweller is trained not to make mistakes. The unremitting cruelty of the desert has bred the qualities that enable him to live with himself. Moreover he has learned to accept infinity and eternity as basic factors in everyday existence.

The man who has never learned to live with himself in solitude is afraid both of himself and of nature. He dares not sit down for a period of contemplative thinking. He can't derive inspiration from watching the majestic glory of a sunset or sitting quietly in the deepening dusk until darkness makes the stars visible.

Few people realize how much time which might otherwise be significantly employed is taken up by the demands of social life in card playing, idle conversation, watching television, or in other activities destined to "pass the time."

The prospector who has spent much time in the desert has learned to relax against the shady side of some unpainted shack and calmly regard the infinity of space with steady eyes while enveloped in silence which stretches down from interstellar space to the surface of the earth. In the understanding of nature, he has come to understand himself.

Looking for wheel tracks while exploring the desert.

Years ago I explored the desert in my camp wagon.

Many a city dweller confronted with similar conditions and an enforced period of silence would at first experience a strange restlessness, then a vague unrest which might well ripen into panic.

The desert is of course constantly shrinking as civilization makes its remorseless inroads. Yet it is surprising how much of the desert remains, silent, inscrutable; and, in places, impenetrable and unchanged. It is a vast source of recreation and mystery lying at your back door.

The Lost Peg-Leg Mine, the Lost Dutchman Mine, the Lost Arch Mine, the Lost Dutch Oven Mine – all these and scores of others bear witness that even modern transportation has not really conquered the desert.

For many years now I have been exploring the desert. First, with a camp wagon – a Chevrolet truck that carried a little house of sorts containing a large supply of drinking water, enough food to last me (in a pinch) for thirty days, a bed with ample cover, and a gasoline cooking stove.

In those days the maximum speed limit was thirty-five miles an hour, there were few paved roads, and my vehicle couldn't be operated at a greater speed than twenty-five miles an hour without burning out a connecting rod bearing. Nevertheless, poking along at twenty-five miles an hour with a compound transmission, I penertated many wild parts of the desert.

Later on, of course, as soon as four-wheel-drive cars became available for civilians, I purchased jeeps. Then I supplemented these with a Land Rover, International four-wheel-drive pickups, and Ford four-wheel-drive pickups on which I have placed camping bodies – a modern de luxe version of my old camp wagon.

A little group of us began to explore the California, Nevada and Arizona deserts. Gradually curiosity got the better of our prudence and we began to take chances, exploring the deserts of Baja California, getting into places where tourists had never been, supplementing our ground forces by bringing in chartered helicopters.

Then we began to wonder what would happen if we used helicopters to explore the desert at will, looking for places where it would be impossible even for four-wheel-drive automobiles to penetrate, landing in the little hidden valleys which were too far from a supply of water to have permitted a prospector to camp there, too inaccessible over rugged mountain ranges for a man and burro to pick a trail. In short, some of the places where we could reasonably assume man had never been – and from which, incidentally, we could never escape if things went wrong.

We felt certain there were many of these places, but how many of them were there, and what would we find if we reached them?

My associates and I debated the point around many a campfire, and then finally decided to find out.

Chapter Four
The Legend of the Lost Peg-Leg Mine

This is a good time to get acquainted with a few of my associates who will be with us from time to time on our desert exploration.

Sam Hicks has been with me for some fourteen years. He is a Wyoming rancher, hunter and outfitter.

During the days when he was guiding hunters and wrangling "dudes" in Wyoming, he was considered even by his competitors to be one of the best elk hunters and all-round outdoor men in the state.

Sam is six-feet-two in height, a stranger to any form of fear or frustration; what he starts to do, he does. He has no fat. Bone, sinew, muscle and brain comprise the equipment with which he copes with life.

He can pick up a two-hundred-and-twenty-five-pound side of meat and toss it up on a pack horse without apparent effort. He can ride all day without showing the faintest sign of fatigue. He has had experience as a "bronc-stomper," is saddle-toughened and can ride just about anything.

Sam is, moreover, a pretty darned good photographer, has

Sam Hicks, a tall mountaineer.

done quite a bit of writing for various magazines, and is a fair-to-middling auto mechanic. Always good-natured, he has a wonderful sense of humor and is an invaluable man on any camping trip.

J. W. Black is an inventive genius, a mechanical wizard, and one of the most rugged individuals I have ever met.

With Black along on an expedition, nothing can go wrong that can't be fixed one way or another; he has worked in machinery all his life.

Heaven knows how he does it, but mechanical emergencies which would be catastrophic to most people are everyday incidents in Black's life. Just as some people have a knack with animals, so Black has a knack with machinery. He can give it a twist here, a tap there, make a few turns with a wrench or screwdriver and the thing starts running and keeps running.

He loves camping and boating, and is an ardent water-skier. His well-proportioned body has just about the most perfect co-ordination I have ever seen. He enjoys life to the limit.

He designed the Pak-Jak, a two-wheeled motor vehicle intended for off-the-road use in almost any sort of rugged terrain, and then followed it up with a smaller, lighter edition called the Burrito.

Jack Hicks, Sam's brother, is a second edition of Sam as far as abilities are concerned and is one of the most even-tempered men I have ever met. I have never seen him when he was even slightly ruffled.

Bill Berry, a tall loose-jointed individual with a whimsical sense of humor, has a philosophical acceptance of all hardships; Joe Templeton, a former partner when I had a sales business, is a well-muscled, chunky chap with a great zest for adventure, and intense loyalty to his friends.

There are others whom we shall meet from time to time

Jack Hicks, expert hunter, tracker and camper.

Bill Berry.

J. W. Black in his workshop at Paradise, California.

and with whom we will get acquainted as they join the expeditions.

When Black came out with the Pak-Jak he was one of the pioneers on the market. By the time he had the Burrito designed and in production the idea had caught on and now there are literally dozens of these motorized scooters which are designed for off-the-road use.

As might be expected, their use has become controversial. Nature lovers who want to keep the outdoors completely primitive and isolated, so that one can find solitude as well as scenery, bitterly resent their use.

The scooter enthusiasts, who are constantly growing in numbers, feel that as part of the public they are entitled to use the public domain.

There are many things to be said on both sides.

I personally am standing somewhat with a foot in each camp. I have done a lot of back-packing and love it. On the

Joe Templeton.

other hand, I have done quite a bit of exploring by motor scooter and love that.

There is a lot of out-of-doors and if the various parties will be reasonable, its use can be regulated in such a way that there will be room for all and each can find amusement to his liking.

The situation is somewhat similar to the use of outboard motors. The lake dweller who has built a mansion on the shores of a lake would like to sleep late on Sunday morning. He is exasperated at the sound of outboard motors.

The fisherman who has arisen at daylight and gone to some secluded cove where he can cast a plug for bass, bitterly resents the water skiers who come roaring by at thirty miles an hour, sending up waves which rock his boat and frighten the fish.

Yet somehow everyone seems to get along, enjoying himself in his own way.

It would be unthinkable to exclude all motorboats from the public lakes because the householder wants to sleep late on Sunday morning. It would be unthinkable to prohibit a person from fishing because his presence interfered with water skiers, and it would be unfair to prohibit water skiing because other people wanted to fish.

As it is, the courteous water skier, seeing a man in a boat fishing, tries to give him a reasonably wide area of undisturbed water.

Of course, there are exceptions. Sometimes water skiers are selfish and inconsiderate. But when one realizes the amount of business that has been developed by the outboard motor, the boats on trailers and the amount of enjoyment the public gets from using the waterways, one must realize what a tragedy it would have been if the early protests of the persons who objected to outboard motors had resulted in restrictive legislation.

The development of the motorized off-the-road scooter is allowing many thousands of persons who had never been able to enjoy the outdoors before to get into the wilderness. It is giving employment to a good many people and is building up a lot of small businesses and some which are not small at all.

I well remember our first trip into the desert by Pak-Jak. J. W. Black had conceived the idea of a motorized scooter with a large rear wheel, a gear reduction which would enable it to move slowly over any type of obstacle but with a clutch that would enable it to speed up to ten or fifteen miles an hour when the going was good.

We had planned a desert trip to give this machine a thorough testing and had arranged for a start early in the year when the air would be crisp and bracing, the nights reasonably cool, and the daytime temperatures not much over eighty-five or ninety.

However, as is always the case with manufacturing anything new, certain "bugs" developed, which J. W. had to eliminate, and week by week, then day by day we would get bulletins from him telling us that the machines were coming along fine but we would have to postpone the trip for another "few days."

As it finally turned out, Black got the machines finished and arrived at my ranch in Temecula the first part of May, which was altogether too late for desert exploration — at least in comfort.

However, the weather had kept cool and we had great hopes of being able to have at least one trip before it became unbearably hot. It had generally been our idea to take a tentative look for the Lost Peg-Leg Mine. This was, of course, more or less of an excuse. We didn't really expect to find the Lost Peg-Leg Mine, but we did expect to have a whale of a good time looking for it.

Some of the original buildings at Warner Springs are still standing.

I presume most of my readers are familiar with the story of this legendary figure of Peg-Leg Smith and the fabulous riches he discovered, but it may not be amiss to take a brief glance at the story and try to separate the facts of history from the fiction of fancy.

There can be little doubt that the mine exists. As an ex-lawyer accustomed to viewing the testimony of witnesses with a certain amount of skepticism, however, I personally am convinced that the story Peg-Leg Smith told, which was supposed to be helpful in enabling others to find the mine, actually introduced a certain element of confusion into the search.

There is of course no good reason why a mature man in full possession of his faculties, being in a position where he could not immediately return to the desert to develop a fabulously rich gold deposit he had stumbled upon, should be so co-operative as to give specific directions to all and sundry so that they could locate the mine before he was able to get started on a return trip.

The Legend of the Lost Peg-Leg Mine

Personally I don't think Peg-Leg Smith was as simple or as naïve as some of the legends indicate.

In any event, Peg-Leg Smith is supposed to have arrived at the Warner Ranch, literally dragged along by a horse that was almost as exhausted as the man.

The date is supposed to have been 1853.

There was something like ten thousand dollars worth of gold in the saddlebags. The stories all agree that this gold was black. It consisted of wind-and-water-worn nuggets covered with a black coating.

The most authentic accounts I have been able to find state that cowboys from the Warner Ranch came upon a horse slowly plodding along a series of flats to the west of Sentenac Canyon. Since the horse appeared at first glance to be riderless, the cowboys rode up to investigate.

They found a man walking on the shady side of the animal, his hands clasped in a final frenzy to the horn of the saddle; the man's eyes were glazed, his lips swollen, and his hands were cracked by parching heat.

The building in which Peg-Leg Smith recovered from his desert experience.

The cowboys tried to talk to the man but he was unable to comprehend what they said. They poured cooling water on his face and chest, finally got him to take a drink, loaded him in a wagon and got him to Warner Springs.

When they unsaddled the horse they found that the saddlebags were filled with what appeared to be smooth black pebbles which were unusually heavy.

The man had a peg leg and had evidently been in the desert for a long time.

It is an interesting fact, apparently well authenticated, that when the cowboys tried to give the horse water he drank only a few gulps. Evidently the horse had found water after his master had become too delirious to recognize the presence of the life-giving fluid.

It was several days before the man emerged from delirium. Then he give his name as Smith and identified himself only as Peg-Leg Smith.

The black pebbles, of course, turned out to be gold covered with an arsenic substance of some sort. Peg-Leg Smith, being unable to travel and being subjected to searching inquiry as to where he had discovered the gold, freely answered all questions, asking only that when the searchers located the rich deposit they would give him half.

Of course everyone promised, and Smith repeatedly told a story of starting from the present location of Yuma, Arizona, getting lost, finding three black buttes and climbing to the top of one of them to see if he could get his bearings and locate some trace of water. He went on to say that the level ground at the top of the butte he had climbed was carpeted with these round black pebbles which were so heavy he decided to investigate. So he simply loaded up his saddlebags and traveled on.

The rich gold strike caused a flare of excitement and literally hundreds of people at one time or another have gone out into the desert searching for the three black buttes (some versions have it there are only two black buttes) and the black gold of Peg-Leg Smith.

Legend also has it that after Peg-Leg Smith got well and was able to travel he returned to the desert trying to find his mine.

Here the stories again are in sharp contradiction. Some say that Smith was never able to find his mine until he made his final trip from which he never returned. A trapper showed up with a story of finding the badly decomposed body of a one-legged man with leather sacks containing huge quantities of gold. The trapper had picked up all he could carry and finally made his way to civilization. He returned with other people trying to find the body but they were never able to find it. They did, however, prospect around in the vicinity.

This story has some semblance of foundation because of other legends that years later, and in the general vicinity where the body was supposed to have been located, a man found a hand whittled wooden leg of the exact type used by Peg-Leg Smith. Not recognizing the significance of his discovery, however, and because the wood was badly weather-worn the man didn't bring the peg leg back with him and didn't mark the place where he had found it.

By a process of deduction and elimination, coupled perhaps with a knowledge of the type of topography which would be consistent with the three black buttes, searchers originally fanned out through the Cocopah Mountains (just south of Signal Hill, which is to the west of Mexicali).

Later on, however, Peg-Leg searchers who had more of an opportunity to analyze Smith's story decided that he had come through the Superstition Mountains, a very barren, sandy, desolate range on the extreme west end of the Imperial Valley (not to be confused with the Superstition

Mountains east of Phoenix, the location of the Lost Dutchman Mine).

In later years students who have found where Smith started his journey have become increasingly skeptical.

Apparently Smith started from a point to the north of the Chemehuevi Mountains. He *said* he reached the junction of the Gila and Colorado rivers (the present location of Yuma). If this story were true, however, he would have had to go some eighteen miles to the east simply in order to go back eighteen miles to the west.

The logical route for him to have taken was a much more northerly one, and Smith is reported to have told a friend in his later years that all the searchers for his mine had been thirty miles too far to the south.

There is, however, one clue to the location of the Peg-Leg Smith Mine which has been overlooked, and which may be of major importance to its eventual discovery.

Starting with the assumption that Peg-Leg Smith did not take the route he said he did, but instead took the more logical one through the Chocolate Mountains, bringing him out somewhere around the present northern edge of the Salton Sea, we can check his line of travel within a few miles.

In later years Smith is reported to have told a friend about encountering a series of mud volcanoes. Almost without question Smith was referring to the mud pots to the south of Niland in a spot now covered by the Salton Sea. (These mud pots were like miniature volcanoes scattered over a considerable distance, and they presented a startling sight as boiling-hot mud bubbled out of their craters. See pages 48, 49.)

But the key clue to the location of the Peg-Leg Smith Mine probably lies in the story of the Lost Squaw Mine.

Horace West, who made as careful a study of the famous

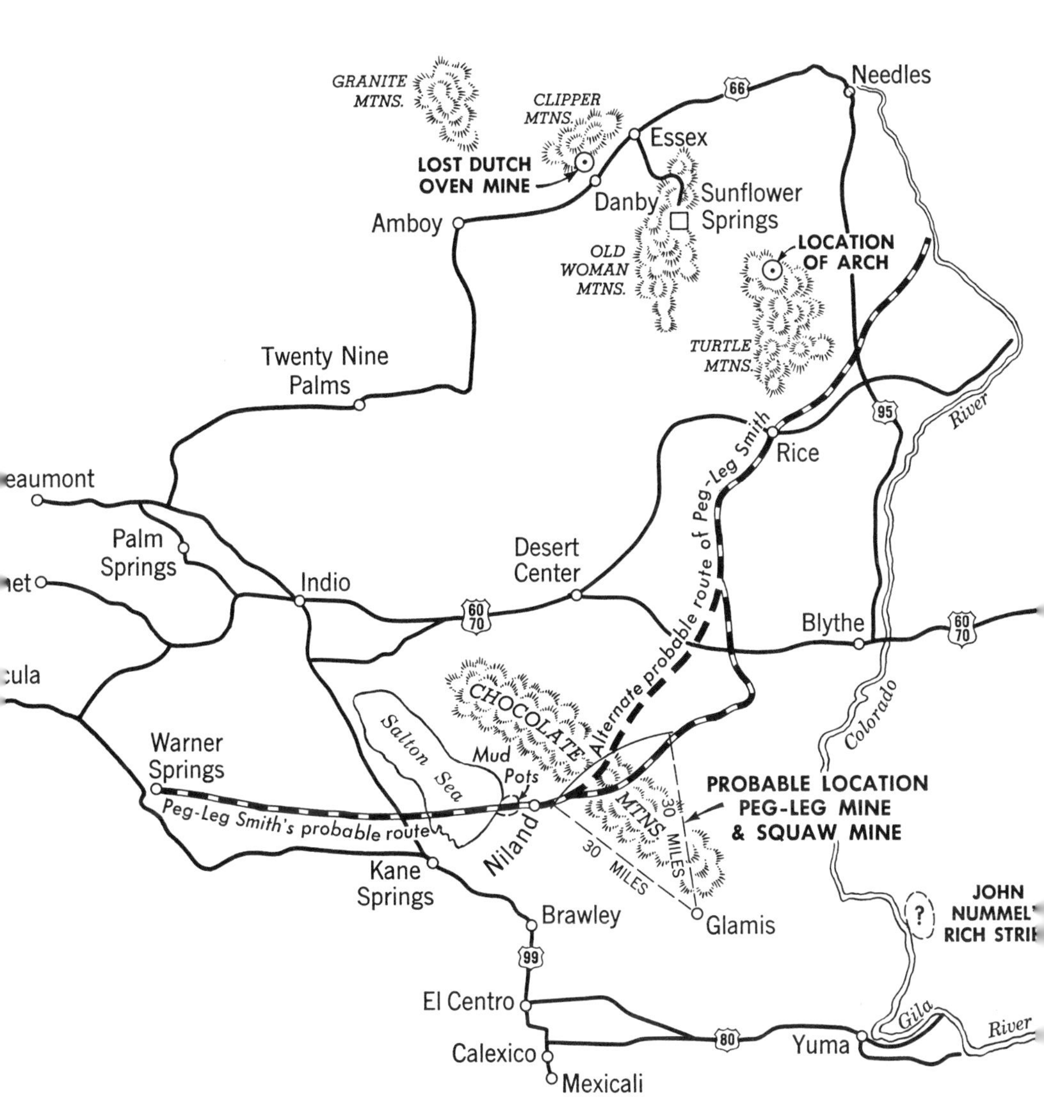

Probable locale of Lost Peg-Leg Mine.

lost mines as anyone, tells the story of the Lost Squaw Mine in his *Miner's Guide.*

Briefly, it goes as follows:

Shortly after the turn of the century, the Southern Pacific Railroad was doing considerable work in the Imperial Valley, and had a large crew stationed between Ogleby and Salton.

In those days the locomotives were all driven by steam

From left to right: the author and Mahlon Vail ask Teofilo Helm, one of the old inhabitants, about the exact location of the buildings at Warner Springs.

and it was necessary to have watering tanks at various places along the track. This was particularly true in the Imperial Valley, where temperatures get to a hundred and twenty in the shade day after day.

One of these watering stations was near Glamis, where there was a tank with a spout for watering locomotives, and down below the tank there was a pipe with a faucet and a little trough filled with water.

One terribly hot day a crew was working on the track to the north of Glamis when they saw an Indian squaw carrying something, and walking slowly toward the trough.

Being busy with what they were doing, the crew had not noticed her until she drew near the tracks. Apparently she had come from the Chocolate Mountains, to the north and east.

The crew watched her as she approached the water, drank copiously and spilled it over her hair, face and shoulders. She was suffering acutely from lack of water and the excessive heat had driven her to a point near delirium.

Thinking they might assist her, the foreman and one other member of the crew started down the track toward the watering trough. As soon as the squaw saw them coming, she got to her feet and with superhuman effort began a staggering run as fast as she could go down the track and in the opposite direction.

Realizing that they were only doing a disservice by trying to aid her, the men returned to their work.

The squaw left the tracks and turned back toward the Chocolate Mountains. Once or twice she hesitated, as though debating with herself, then kept on traveling.

It wasn't until sometime later that the men approached the place where the squaw had been drinking, and there for the first time saw part of a blanket, its four corners knotted to form a sack.

It was very heavy. When they untied it, they found it entirely filled with smooth nuggets, ranging in size from that of a dime to that of an English walnut and all coated with a black substance which was paper-thin, yet strong and tenacious. Scratched with a knife, the nuggets revealed pure gold of darkest hue.

The men tried to follow the squaw, some of them wanting to return the gold, others desirous of finding the place from which the gold had been taken, but as they came to a harder, rocky surface in the desert they lost her tracks entirely.

The similarity between the gold found by Peg-Leg Smith and that found by the Indian squaw is too striking to be overlooked.

The Indian squaw was on foot. She was carrying no provisions, no canteen. She had come from the direction of the Chocolate Mountains. It is hardly possible that she had come from a point more than one day's journey away.

Starting, therefore, at Glamis, making a sector into the Chocolate Mountains, we can cover the probable route of the squaw. And we find that this route intersects that of the probable route of Peg-Leg Smith.

It is my opinion that when the Peg-Leg Mine is eventually rediscovered, it will be found in the area indicated on the map on page 85. And I would not be too surprised to find that the three buttes were completely nonexistent and the gold came from a prehistoric water course on what is now perhaps a plateau above the numerous channels which have been washed by cloudbursts in the Chocolate Mountains.

Searching for some of these lost mines in the desert is like looking for the proverbial needle in a haystack. In the case of others, the development of modern transportation has opened up tempting opportunities.

My friend, Mahlon Vail, a prosperous cattleman, was

familiar with Warner Springs in his boyhood some sixty years ago. He, Teofilo Helm, a boyhood companion who has lived on or near Warner's Ranch all his life, and I prowled the Warner ranch searching for some of the old landmarks.

The place is steeped in tradition, and the aura of the early days still clings to the old dobe house.

We were able to reconstruct some of the environment of the famous Peg-Leg Smith, but the passing of time has obliterated some of the earlier clues. We had hoped to find someone who had heard the Peg-Leg Mine story from someone who in turn had heard it first hand.

Despite the rich memories of earlier days which we uncovered, we couldn't get back far enough to discover any new angle on the famous lost mine.

The place has been formally declared an historic landmark, but this has not stopped treasure seekers from tearing out the fireplace or vandals from scratching their names all over the walls.

We found that even fifty or sixty years ago, there was a haze of uncertainty hanging over the old landmark as to exactly where the Butterfield Stage made its stop, how long the store had been in its then location and certain other factors.

It is, therefore, not surprising that so many details of the story concerning Peg-Leg Smith should have become obscured in a similar haze of antiquity.

There is also another lost mine we are going to be searching for, the Lost Arch Mine. Since that mine has made periodic appearances in my life for the last thirty-odd years, it may be in order to take a look at its legend in the next chapter.

Chapter Five
A Scheme to Find the Lost Arch Mine

My first connection with the Lost Arch Mine was the result of a peculiar combination of interests. I was interested in a principle of optics used to penetrate camouflage, and I was interested in some of the famous lost mines of the Southwest.

These two interests were brought together by the Lost Arch Mine.

As far back as World War I, the military began to experiment with camouflage. During the years this became very much of a science. It became virtually impossible to detect certain small objects from the air, once those objects had been covered by a protective camouflage.

Then the other side tried to find some method of penetrating this camouflage and destroying its military value. The result was an ingenious application of certain natural principles in the field of optics.

Human powers of observation are assisted by the spacing of approximately three inches between man's eyes. Man sees an image with each eye and fuses those images so that he has an angle of "perspective" and in that way is able to judge distance.

It is surprising that a base line of no more than three inches enables a man to judge distance so accurately. The trained hunter can readily distinguish range so that he can tell whether to adjust his sights for three hundred yards, four hundred yards or five hundred yards.

So inventive genius began to speculate about what would happen if the base line between the two eyes should be increased and then, by means of optical devices, views taken from each base line could be fused together just as the two eyes fuse what they normally see.

By careful experimentation it was found that a base line of one in ten could be used in this manner and the vision could still be fused by the aid of optical instruments.

In other words, by sending a photographer up in an airplane to a height of ten thousand feet, having him fly a straight course, take photographs at regular intervals, then move to the side for one thousand feet on a parallel course and again take photographs at regular intervals, the prints of these photographs could be put in frames with mirrors at carefully calculated angles so that the two views could be fused.

Anyone who has never seen such a stereosurvey would be astounded at what happens.

There is, of course, an exaggerated effect of height. A building fifty feet high seems to be stretching up some five hundred feet, a matter of interest to the military observer. For instance, suppose a bridge spanning a river was so skillfully camouflaged that even the most careful inspection failed to disclose it. Under a stereophotographic process the bridge would become plainly visible, not as a bridge, but as a part of the river which seemed to throw a narrow band some hundred feet above the surface of the water.

This process has now been perfected so that the trained observer can get the height of an object within a matter of inches. A white dot seems to "float" in the field of vision. This dot can be moved by means of a knurled knob so it can be placed on any lateral section of a photograph. Then it can seemingly be raised or lowered. It can be put at the base of a building and then "raised" to the top of the building. Consulting a scale on the moving mechanism will give one the actual height of the structure.

Now, *some* of the famous lost mines in the desert contain physical landmarks which could very easily be evaluated by a system of this sort.

For instance, quite a few of the mines were worked at one time so there would be a tunnel, and in front of the tunnel a graded ore dump.

Where these mines were abandoned because of Indian hostilities or the owners killed and the exact location in doubt, stereophotography of this sort would show up the contours of the mining dump despite the fact that in the course of a hundred years or so the brush will have grown up to such an extent that the human eye in ocular observation could not detect the contours.

The famous Lost Arch Mine is supposed to be marked by a very beautiful natural arch spanning a canyon.

According to legend, the Lost Arch Mine has been twice discovered and twice lost.

One of the best accounts is contained in a somewhat obscure paperback book entitled *The Miner's Guide* published by Horace West nearly fifty years ago.

West was a practical miner and his book contains down-to-earth information for the prospector and miner. I presume it would be next to impossible to obtain a copy now. My own copy is one I have had for years and my records show that thirty years ago I had personal correspondence with

Horace West, who gave me permission to quote from his book.

The story of how I happened to write for that permission is interesting, but before we go into it, let's take a look at the mine's history.

Boiled down to essentials, the Lost Arch Mine goes back almost a hundred years. Two prospectors, Crocker and Fish, equipped with the comparative luxury of a buckboard and horses, were conducting a leisurely prospecting trip in the desert. They had left Nevada and were working their way to California.

In the buckboard they hauled a barrel of water in addition to their essential camping equipment, and from time to time the men would fill their canteens from this barrel of water.

One morning Fish tilted the barrel and was astounded to find it was almost empty. Investigation disclosed it had sprung a leak.

A swift examination showed that there was barely enough left in the barrel to make a half-canteen of water.

These men were hardened prospectors. They knew what the mishap meant. It was virtually the same as a sentence of death. They had a hurried conference and decided that it would probably be impossible to get back to the Colorado River before dying of thirst and as far as they knew, the Colorado River was their nearest source of water.

They discussed the fact that there could well be some springs or at least potholes in the mountains a lot nearer than the Colorado. The only trouble was they didn't know anything about the topography of the country or where such sources of water might be found.

After thinking things over, they decided to put in half a day exploring on foot, trying to find water. Then they would rendezvous back at the wagon. If they hadn't found water, they would then try making a dash for the Colorado. This plan not only gave them the chance of finding water closer to their camp and so spare them making the forced march to the river, but it meant that if they did have to make that fearsome journey, they could start in the cooler part of the day with the comparative coolness of the night ahead of them. Plodding their way through the hot deep sand in the intense heat of the day would be suicidal. And, in any event, their chances of reaching the Colorado River were slim and they knew it.

It was therefore agreed that the partners would separate, each search for water until noon, and then return to camp. If they had been unsuccessful they would then start their journey to the river.

Pursuant to this understanding, the men started out, Crocker taking a canyon on the left, Fish taking the canyon to the right.

Fish worked his way up a canyon around huge granite boulders, some of them as big as a house.

This water-washed canyon had been caused by the torrential summer cloudbursts which bring "flash floods" to the desert.

The heat was intense and there was no sign of water. Plodding his way up the canyon, Fish found the going exceedingly difficult.

He was never able to tell exactly how far he went. It is hard to estimate distances under such conditions, but Fish did go until he was nearly exhausted. He was, of course, trying to cover just as much ground as possible in the shortest period of time.

He found no water but just as he was about to turn back, he noticed a place where a natural arch bridged the canyon some distance ahead. He determined to go as far as this arch and then rest in the shade cast by it. Downhill progress would be much swifter, and he could still get back to camp at the appointed time.

So Fish forced himself on until he came to this natural arch and then flung himself down in the shade cast by it.

The ground was comparatively cool there, and Fish, physically tired, mentally apprehensive as he thought of the race with death ahead, was torn with emotion as he sucked in deep lungfuls of heated air.

The sun, hitting the side of the canyon walls and reflecting down, had so heated the air that after exertion it was hard to get life-giving oxygen from it.

It was then that Fish pushed his hands deep into the cool gravel, trying to relieve his throbbing wrists. As he did so he noticed something peculiar about the dirt.

Scooping up a handful, he started blowing away the lighter particles and found that he had a whole palmful of gold.

Tremendously excited, Fish started picking up handfuls of dirt, blowing away the lighter portions, putting the heavier grains of gold in his pocket.

Now, it is here that the cautious or perhaps the skeptical observer begins to question the story. If enough water during periods of flood had been roaring down that canyon so that great boulders could be dislodged and worn by water, why would alluvial gold the size of wheat grains be on the *surface* of the ground?

Yet there they were, and the proof lies in the fact that Fish came back with his pockets full of gold which he had secured in a short period of time simply by blowing on light gravel he had scooped up with his hands. He had no other means available.

Is it possible that there was a very rich deposit on the side of the canyon just a short distance above where Fish had flung himself down in the cool canyon to rest?

As a prospector who knew something about hunting for gold, Fish should certainly have ascertained where that gold came from. And a very short period of exploration would have given him the answer.

But Fish had pressed on to the farthest limit of distance and endurance, and he was going to have to hurry back down the canyon in order to reach his camp in time for the rendezvous with his partner. He had picked up gold and filled his pockets but he didn't have any time to waste prospecting around.

What about his pockets? History doesn't say.

Under the circumstances Fish would hardly have been wearing a coat, so the probabilities are that in filling his pants pockets with gold he had a rather limited supply.

The day was hot and Fish was already feeling the pangs of thirst, the first symptoms of the life-and-death struggle that was to ensue. So he hurried back down the dry watercourse, and was only a few minutes late in joining his partner at the camp.

Fish told his partner about the gold he had found. They were rich!

But you can't drink gold, and as the two men realized in sober appraisal of the situation, their chances of ever getting out alive were rather slim.

Under the circumstances it is completely understandable that they would concentrate their attention on the best way of getting to water, lightening the vehicle as much as possible, making a "dash" for the Colorado.

So they started. And one can appreciate their mental condition, their apprehension, their near-panic as they started that long, almost hopeless journey.

That near-panic is undoubtedly the reason they didn't pay too much attention to landmarks. At the moment their chances of being alive long enough to try finding their way

Cactus spines give a soft appearance which is deceptive. These thorns are sharp as needles, hard as spikes.

Joshua palms.

A hundred rich lost mines could hide in terrain such as this. Taken from helicopter while exploring the Turtle Range of mountains.

Weird colorings in desert mountains.

The winter rains are normal but sometimes very rare. After normal winter rains (as distinguished from flash floods) the desert blooms.

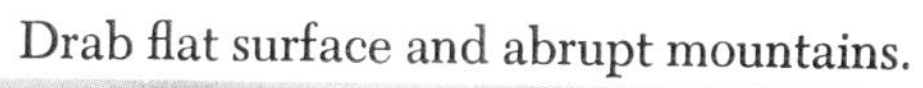

Drab flat surface and abrupt mountains.

At times the canyons are bordered by sheer walls of hard rock.

House trailers in the high desert country make for healthful living.

back didn't seem hopeful and they were concentrating on reaching the life-giving water of the Colorado rather than finding their way back.

The journey was a nightmare, the horses begging for water, the men dying of thirst with no water to offer.

At length, after interminable hours of slogging through sand and heat, groping their way through darkness, the horses began to smell water. They called on their reserve strength and staggered to the banks of the Colorado River.

The men fell into the cool waters, drinking sparingly at first, letting their parched, tortured skins soak up the refreshing fluid.

Fish, who was in better shape after they had rested, took Crocker on to Ehrenberg for medical treatment, but the man died within a few days of his arrival.

Fish spent several weeks, first recuperating and then getting ready to start back for his fabulously rich gold deposit.

He was, of course, indefinite about stating where the deposit was located, simply that it was somewhere in the Old Woman Mountains.

The Old Woman Mountains is a rough range of mountains, with boulder-strewn canyons, barren ridges of rock, great slabs of upthrust granite and in general a forbidding appearance.

The range derives its name from a towering granite figure which has been carved by the elements so that it bears a startling resemblance to an old woman silhouetted against the skyline on the very crest of the mountains. This granite figure is visible for miles and is so realistic that it furnishes a name for the whole range.

Although it is quite possible that Fish made his story about the location of the gold deposit deliberately indefinite, or perhaps downright misleading, the fact is that Fish went back to the Old Woman Mountains. He went back again and

The Old Woman Mountains get their name from a peculiar rock formation resembling a brooding old woman.

again and again, but he was never able to find even the camp from which they had started, let alone the canyon with the natural arch spanning it.

So far, so good. This is one of the typical stories of lost mines.

When one begins to examine it with a skeptical eye there are several things about it that are all but incomprehensible, but the partners had the gold to prove their story.

Alluvial gold with water-worn nuggets the size of wheat grains furnishes evidence that simply can't be ignored, nor can one discount the fact that Fish spent all the money he was ever able to get, and the rest of his life, in a vain search for his mine, going back time after time to the Old Woman range of mountains.

Now let's look at the second chapter of this fascinating story.

A Scheme to Find the Lost Arch Mine

Directly to the east of the Old Woman range of mountains, and just a little to the south, lies a somewhat smaller range, the Turtle Mountains.

It must be remembered that these desert mountain ranges are very similar in appearance. The mountains rise up to a great height, consisting largely of piles of rock, covered here and there with a thin layer of soil made by decomposing rock and the remnants of vegetation of a bygone age. There is just enough soil to furnish a foothold for cacti, greasewood and sagebrush. The crests are jagged and cruel and, even when they are softened somewhat by distance, appear formidable and forbidding.

Fish had made his discovery in 1883. He spent the rest of his life in a vain search. By 1900 he was dead and the Lost Arch Mine had become one of the legends of the West. Prospectors had searched for it, and searched in vain.

At the turn of the century a prospector named John Packer

Typical desert scenery.

had been out prospecting in the desert and had explored the terrain until he found it necessary to head back to the city in order to replenish his supplies.

In those days, if a prospector was successful he had enough gold to buy provisions. If he hadn't been successful he had to return to the settlements, work at a job, and save enough money to get the few necessities required to start on another prospecting trip.

Packer hadn't been successful and was headed north, toward Needles, where he planned to get a job that would enable him to build up another "stake."

He had made an early camp and had a cheery fire blazing away in the dusk, when he became aware that someone was approaching.

The man who came up to the campfire explained that his name was Kohler, that he was a German naturalist who had decided to come to the West because of stories of riches to be had for the taking in the desert mountains.

Packer invited Kohler to unroll his blankets and spend the night with him.

They had a frugal supper and then sat talking, each prospector, after his fruitless search, hungry for the sound of a human voice and the pleasure of companionship. The lonely vigils they had been spending in the desert made them unusually communicative as they sat around the flickering fire.

Kohler was apologetic. As a naturalist he should have done better. He had found some very likely-looking prospects, some places that he wanted to develop and which he thought were going to become rich mines, but he hadn't come on any alluvial gold which would enable him to buy provisions. He, too, was going to have to go to some settlement and work to get a stake. He announced that he was headed for Amboy. He had heard there was plenty of employment there. It was

We camped at the foot of a weird rock formation which contained Indian petroglyphs.

There is always the temptation to linger over breakfast.

a point on the railroad where considerable lumber was being shipped for mining purposes and construction.

So, in turn, each man gave a little summary of his prospecting trip, of his hopes and disappointments and plans for the future.

They had about talked themselves out. The fire had died to a bed of barely glowing embers, and the men were preparing to turn in, when Kohler mentioned an incidental matter which had interested him as a naturalist.

He had, he said, been on a mesa which had a slope to the north, and from that point he had seen a natural arch spanning a canyon. He said that he was very much interested in the arch but, being primarily interested in his prospecting, hadn't taken the time to examine the arch closely. He wanted to do this sometime when he was on another trip with a little more time.

It was quite apparent to Packer that the German naturalist had never heard of the Lost Arch Mine.

A Scheme to Find the Lost Arch Mine

Packer concealed his excitement, yawned a couple of times, stretched, took a stick, musingly stirred the coals and then said, in effect, "Look, we've been thrown together by Fate. We're both of us going back to earn a stake and then return to do some propecting. It's pretty lonely prospecting by one's self. You have knowledge as a naturalist and I have practical experience as a prospector. Why don't we go into partnership?"

Kohler was pleased with the idea and instantly accepted.

The two men shook hands on the bargain.

It was agreed that Kohler would go to Amboy and get a job, that Packer would go to Needles and get a job there. They were then to meet at Sunflower Springs twenty days later.

Packer got his job in Needles, saved his money, got a stake, returned to Sunflower Springs. But Kohler failed to show up. After waiting several days Packer became alarmed and went to Amboy to try and find some trace of his partner.

At the extreme lower left is the building at Sunflower Springs, the fenced enclosure, and, to the right of the building, Tom Farley's distinctive car.

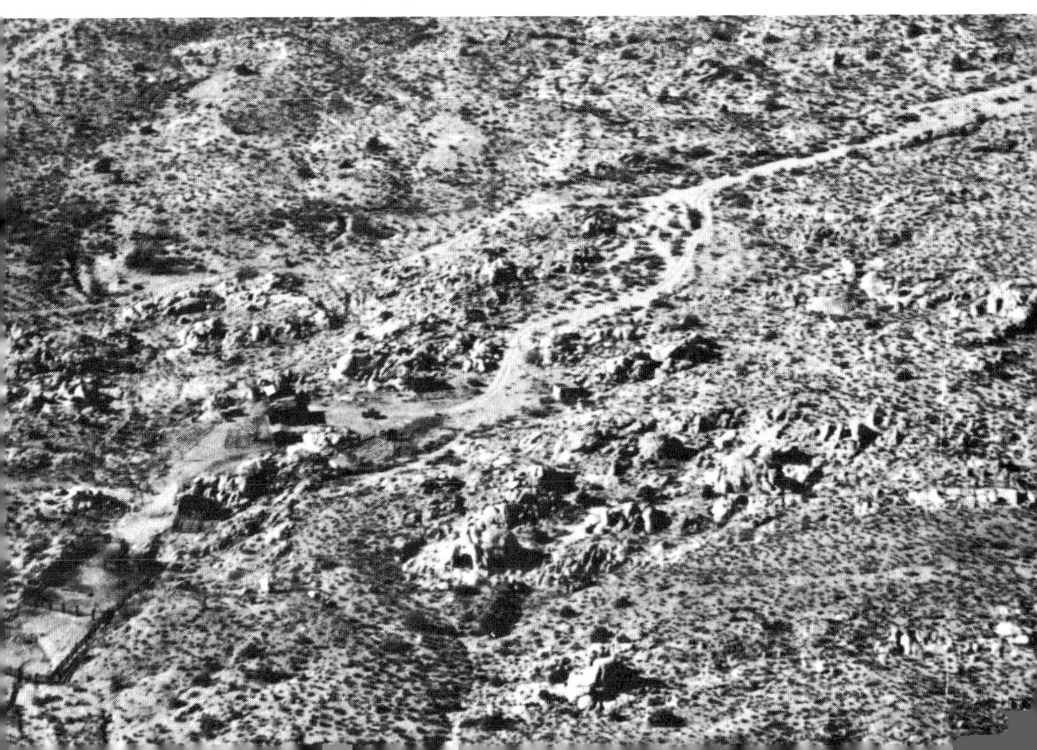

He learned that Kohler had reached Amboy and gotten a job unloading carloads of lumber, but on the third day a pile of heavy timbers had unexpectedly toppled over, trapping Kohler beneath them and killing him.

So the Lost Arch Mine becomes rather unique in history because it has been twice found and twice lost.

Let's review the salient facts. The original discoverers of the mine were traveling in an old-fashioned buckboard and were en route from Nevada to San Bernardino, making a leisurely prospecting trip. They had filled their barrel with water at the Colorado River and then had gone on for two days in a somewhat haphazard way, instead of following a compass course. So they could easily have been confused as to their location.

If they had been on the east slope of the Turtle Mountains, an air line distance to the Colorado River would have been around twenty-five miles. If they had been on the east slope of the Old Woman Mountains, an air line to the Colorado River would have been approximately forty-five miles, assuming that they left the Sacramento Mountains to the north and the Turtle Mountains to the south as they headed for the river.

Analyzing the evidence, and knowing they had filled the barrel at the Colorado River two days before the camp where they ran out of water, it would seem that they must have been on the eastern slope of the Turtle Mountains or the eastern slope of the Old Woman range. If they had made a forced march from the west side of the Old Woman Mountains, around either the northern or southern end and *then* reached the Colorado, a forced march *might* have enabled them to cover the ground. But two days of rather leisurely prospecting would hardly have got them to a camp on the western side of the Old Woman Mountains.

If they had been on the easterly side of the Old Woman

Mountains, they must have been on the northern half. Sunflower Springs is some twelve or fifteen miles from the northern tip of the Old Woman range and coming from the Colorado River, Fish and Packer would have come on Sunflower Springs if they had worked their way south along the Old Woman Mountains. If that had been the case there would have been no need for their march to the Colorado.

So much for the physical evidence.

Following the report of Kohler's discovery and his death, search for the Lost Arch Mine centered in the Turtle Mountains and it was naturally assumed that Fish had been mistaken in believing that he and his partner had been camped in the Old Woman Mountains.

It must be remembered that in those days it was a difficult matter to get out into the desert on trips of exploration. There were no surfaced roads, no automobiles. The man who wanted to explore was limited to a speed of two or three miles an hour and dared not get very far from some known source of water.

It is therefore not surprising that in the course of a few years the Lost Arch Mine faded from public attention and became merely another legend.

My own interest in the Lost Arch Mine goes back some thirty-five years.

Around 1927 or 1928 I was writing a series of stories for the so-called pulp magazines, dealing with all sorts of wild adventure.

At that time, casting about for new ideas, it occurred to me that if some person would use this technique of stereophotography with an exaggerated base line, it might be possible to discover some of the old lost mines, or at least uncover some interesting clues as to their location.

The Lost Arch Mine seemed a natural.

So I started a story dealing with a group of adventurers

The mountain is studded with old mines which our party explores.

who financed themselves by discovering lost mines. They were of course impecunious but handsome, brave and virile. They had a plane and cameras, and the leader was in love with a beautiful girl whose socially prominent parents disapproved of him because he had no money; and naturally there was a rival, the offspring of a very wealthy family, the members of which were typical social snobs.

The plot might have been anticipated. The girl was persuaded by some last minute "derring do" on the part of the hero to cast her lot with the impecunious but attractive male lead of the story, whom she really loved. The socially prominent heir was left waiting at the church, and just as the happy but impoverished young couple prepared to enter upon a life of financial privation, the hero's assistant fused the stereoscopic photographs together and there was the Lost Arch standing out in bold relief.

They went to the location on their honeymoon, filled shoulder packs with gold, located a claim, became exceedingly wealthy and lived happily ever afterward, loaning the girl's family enough to save her father's business when a depression came along.

In those days I was one of the large quantity producers in the world of fiction. There were half a dozen or so of us in the million-word-a-year class who hammered away at our typewriters and kept a steady stream of manuscripts in the mail.

The going rate was three cents a word, and in order to increase income we typed lots of words.

It was a man-killing job, and I mean it was literally a man-killing job. I am just about the only one left of that company whose names appeared week after week on the covers of the pulps.

I was handicapped by the fact that I was a fairly successful trial lawyer and the practice of my legal profession required that I be at the office from nine until five. So my story writing was done late at night and early in the morning.

Toward the last, when my commitments to the magazines required that I have a novelette in the mail every third day, I would dash home from the law office, grab a hasty bite to eat, climb the stairs to my study, start pounding the typewriter, dictate business correspondence to a secretary who was holding down two jobs in order to make both ends meet; then back for another session at the typewriter until one or two o'clock in the morning.

I would then get three or four hours' fitful sleep and arise to write for another two or three hours before breakfast.

Moreover, I kept up this pace for more than ten years, during which I averaged a novelette in the mail every third day in addition to the demands of the law practice.

So it was rather late at night when my friend and former business associate, Joe Templeton, who was driving through Ventura, saw a light in my study and dropped in to tell me I was working too hard and that I was killing myself.

This was old stuff in those days. All of my friends were telling me that. I would listen to them patiently until after they had left to go home and to bed. Then I would return to my interrupted chore of pounding the typewriter.

I listened patiently to Templeton.

After Templeton finished telling me that I was headed for an early appointment with the undertaker, he asked me what story I was working on now, his interest aroused by the profusion of books dealing with the famous lost mines of the West, which were scattered about my study.

So I explained to Joe what I had in mind and told him that I would have the story finished by two or three o'clock that morning.

Joe became tremendously excited. The idea appealed to him as being practical and moreover he knew a man who had some planes at his disposal and who was engaged in stereoscopic map making.

In those days one didn't simply pick up a telephone and say that he wanted to charter a plane at so much an hour to fly over the Turtle Mountains.

Now, Joe Templeton is quite a salesman. For three years or so he and I ran a manufacturer's agency, covering all the territory west of the Rockies, and we made a very good thing of it.

Joe sold me then and there on the idea of actually rediscovering the Lost Arch Mine, rather than having the fictional hero win the mine and the girl.

So, reluctantly I ratcheted the paper out of the typewriter, put the story in a "hold" file and told Joe to go ahead and see what he could do.

Joe left the next morning filled with enthusiasm and I began laboriously to plot another story on buried treasure.

In those days, faced with the necessity of getting out a story every third day, about thirty minutes was all the time I could spare for a plot.

Joe Templeton inspects the sharp, pointed leaf of typical desert foliage.

Those pulp magazines were an institution in themselves. There has never been anything quite like them and probably there never will be again. They are gone now and so are the people who wrote for them; at least the real quantity producers, the aristocrats of the field who made more than twenty to twenty-five thousand dollars a year hammering out words and thinking up plots.

Fortunately I was able to "graduate" before the pulps died a natural death.

Many of the pulp writers graduated to the "slicks." Many of them went down with the ship.

My own graduation was due to the persistence of my agent, Robert Thomas Hardy, and the perspicacity of Thayer Hobson, at that time president of William Morrow & Company, now chairman of the board.

One month, having reached my quota of a hundred thousand words of fiction early enough to give me a little spare time before starting next month's allotment of fiction, I dashed off a mystery novel.

Undaunted by the fact that the book publisher to whom it was submitted promptly rejected it, I found myself again ahead of my quota and wrote another mystery novel. It was also rejected.

Robert Thomas Hardy, however, believed there was something to these books, and after they had been rejected by other publishers, took the manuscripts under his arm and went down to Thayer Hobson's office, making a sales pitch directly to the president of the company and insisting that Hobson read the manuscripts personally.

Hobson read them, and felt that by revising the manuscripts I could make something of them. He particularly wanted to have them tied into a series and have the protagonist a character who could run on for a series.

So, following his suggestion, I revised the manuscripts and created the character of Perry Mason.

William Morrow & Company brought out the first two Perry Mason books, *The Case of the Velvet Claws,* and *The Case of the Sulky Girl.* Hobson, in a blurb on the dust jacket, predicted that the name "Erle Stanley Gardner" was destined to mean something in the world of mystery fiction.

At that time the great Pooh-Bah of the mystery story was Will Cuppy.

Will Cuppy didn't like the stories, he didn't like me, and I have a very strong suspicion that he didn't like Thayer Hobson or anyone else invading his province to predict that any particular person was going to be a success in the mystery field.

In any event, Cuppy disposed of the books with a scathing criticism and, when the third book came out, delivered himself of an ultimatum which was supposed to bury me for all time. "Gardner," he said, "should study Hammett for dialogue and McGuffy for grammar."

Despite Will Cuppy and several other critics, however, the books began to catch on. The reading public began to follow the adventures of Perry Mason with some interest. Ben Hibbs, for twenty years editor of the *Saturday Evening Post,* but at that time an associate editor of *Country Gentleman,* felt that I could write serials his readers would want. I created "Doug Selby, the D.A." for *Country Gentleman,* and after these stories were serialized, Hobson published them as books and so I was able to ease off on the back-breaking chore of doing a million words of fiction every year for the wood-pulp magazines.

In the meantime, Joe Templeton got in touch with his friend who had the airplanes, and outlined to him the story of the Lost Arch Mine and the possibilities of relocating this mine in the Turtle Mountains by an aerial survey.

Templeton's friend looked up the history of the lost mine and thought the idea was sound. The trouble was that all this investigation took some time. Then there was another delay of several months while Templeton's friend was getting himself in a position to move into the vicinity of the Turtle Mountains and start work.

During this period he met a tragic death, and that was the end of our carefully laid plans.

Templeton, however, insisted that sooner or later we would get someone interested who would make a survey of the Turtle Mountains and rediscover the Lost Arch Mine.

The months became years, the Lost Arch Mine was relegated to the background of my thinking, Ben Hibbs moved up to be the editor of the *Saturday Evening Post,* and Perry Mason proved to be all the gold mine I needed. I began to support the government in the style to which it was rapidly becoming accustomed.

The Lost Arch Mine remained in the back of my mind, however, and every once in a while when Templeton and I would

Ben Hibbs, the famous editor, holding the dog, Benhibbs, which the author named after him.

get together to talk over old times, we'd discuss the Lost Arch Mine and the fact that we had been on the verge of rediscovering it.

By this time there were plenty of planes available for charter service. Landing strips had been put in near enough to the Turtle Mountains so it wouldn't be necessary to construct a landing strip for such a survey, and the whole deal would have been much simpler.

The trouble now, however, was that I didn't have any time. Proctor & Gamble picked up Perry Mason, and had him on radio for ten years or more. It was a daily show, Monday through Friday. Then when radio advertising allotments were decreased almost to the vanishing point by the huge bites taken out of the advertising dollar by television, Proctor & Gamble decided to drop the Perry Mason radio show. This, however, didn't help a bit as far as my time was concerned. Columbia Broadcasting Company stepped into the picture and picked up

Perry Mason for a weekly television feature. My responsibilities pyramided to huge proportions.

It wasn't until a few years ago that I began to realize that time was slipping rapidly through my fingers and that if I ever wanted to enjoy life, I was going to have to begin. It was a lot later than I thought.

By this time, getting any sort of a vacation was tremendously complicated and expensive. I had to keep in almost daily touch with Hollywood and whenever scripts were ready for my approval or suggestions I had to charter airplanes which could deliver them to me within a matter of hours, then rush my comments back to Hollywood.

I looked around to see if I couldn't find some really wild, almost unexplored country where the roads were so terrible the tourists hadn't trampled it to death, yet where the air line distance was short enough for a plane to get there from Hollywood within a few hours.

Baja California, the peninsula stretching south from Tijuana to La Paz, was made to order.

I started exploring Baja California, making arrangements with Francisco Munoz, the famous Mexican pilot, to fly me back and forth and to shuttle scripts both ways in a sort of personal air mail service.

Munoz is a colorful character, a wonderful pilot and he knows his way around Baja California the way a good taxi driver know the city in which he is working. Munoz knows every mountain, every canyon, every air current.

Within the space of a few years Munoz became my friend, my guide and my advisor on all matters pertaining to exploration of Baja California. I have spent many, many hours flying with him over rugged terrain, off the regular air channels, looking down on country which is largely unexplored.

Then I met Bob Boughton of the Hiller Aircraft Corporation and found that this company was coming out from time to time

The helicopter descends to explore a water hole in Baja California.

with new model helicopters and was interested in demonstrating them under the most adverse flying conditions available.

If anyone wants adverse flying conditions, Baja California can furnish them.

Baja California is a wild, rugged country. It is a country of air turbulence and bad roads, yet has primitive charm and great beauty. It has the ultimate in desert country, and it is the scourge of aviators and the dread of helicopter pilots.

When I first tried to charter helicopters from companies that rented them, the owners would greet me with open arms. All I had to do was pay the money and the helicopters would be available. But the minute I mentioned Baja California, their manner underwent a sharp change.

However, Bob Boughton, who was in charge of foreign sales for the Hiller Aircraft Corporation, had enough faith in his product to welcome the idea of trying it out in country that was shunned by others. So I started exploring Baja California by helicopter.

By Baja California, in this instance, I mean the almost unknown interior. The northern part of Baja California with its thriving cities of Mexicali, Tijuana, Ensenada and San Felipe is a tourist's delight and a sportsman's paradise.

The extreme southern part, with La Paz, San Jose del Cabo and some of the luxury hotels now being put up there, is one of the most delightful places to spend a vacation and engage in sport fishing that is absolutely out of this world.

The middle part, however, the vast and terrifying Vizcaino Desert, the rugged mountains to the north of the Three Virgins above Santa Rosalia, the roadless stretch of desert between El Barril and Bahia de Los Angeles, can furnish enough adventure in a month to last the average explorer a lifetime.

I had built up a fleet of four-wheel-drive vehicles by means

Breaking camp in Baja California requires fast work by all hands.

Sometimes it is easier to detour over the Baja California desert than to follow the rutted roads.

of which I could set up base camps in places where there were nearby landing strips. Using these vehicles which are equipped with special tires, power winches and able to carry large quantities of gasoline, water and provisions, we explored country no other motorists had ever seen, and I wrote several books dealing with our adventures.

So it was only only natural that when I once more began to think of exploring country close to home in the desert regions of California, Arizona and Nevada, and when, on one of his visits, Joe Templeton asked why it wouldn't be possible to explore the Turtle Mountains with helicopter and actually find the famous Lost Arch, the idea once more began to germinate.

However, the real reawakening of my interest in lost mines came with J. W. Black's Pak-Jaks, and our first adventure in trying them out in the desert.

Chapter Six
Only 117° in the Shade – But No Shade

In view of our subsequent exciting adventures with airplane and helicopter, that first Pak-Jak trip now seems relatively tame, but since the Pak-Jak is the very foundation of our mobility in the desert, we should give it its proper position in the story.

The helicopter and the airplane are the cavalry to be used in scouting, but when it comes right down to brass tacks the Pak-Jak is the infantry which enables us to move in and consolidate our findings.

As I have mentioned earlier, J. W. Black finally got his machines in such shape that he was willing to give them a try-out. He loaded them onto a pickup and made the six-hundred-mile drive from his place in Paradise down to my ranch in Temecula, arriving on a Sunday afternoon.

We jubilantly arranged to start out into the desert the following morning.

Black unloaded his machines and demonstrated what they

J. W. Black starts up the Turtle Mountains on his Pak-Jak.

could do. It was startling. With the greatest of ease, Black rode up rough slopes so steep that we could hardly negotiate them on foot without using our hands as well as our feet.

Watching him move up those slopes I became excited. Here was something revolutionary. Here was something that was destined to open up a whole vista of new horizons.

Walking is a wonderful exercise but a darned poor means of transportation.

A man can have his breakfast in Los Angeles, step into the upholstered comfort of an air-conditioned automobile, glide over ribbons of smooth concrete highways, listening to music as he travels, or tune in to the account of a championship ball game which is being played two thousand miles away. The glare of the road is cut down by filtered glass. He arrives in San Francisco in time for dinner without any feeling of fatigue.

But the man in the desert who wants to collect rocks five miles away on a slope he can see clearly through the crystal desert air, must trudge through sand for a couple of hours, pick up only a few specimens, and then plod wearily back through the deep sand, arriving in camp pretty well exhausted.

In other words, man's inventiveness in the field of transportation has developed in a lopsided way.

We can strap a man in a vehicle, send him soaring out into space, circumnavigating the globe many times in the course of twenty-four hours, and then effect a landing at a predetermined spot.

But when we want to collect rocks in country too rough for a jeep, we are back to the same means of transportation we used ten thousand years ago. Walking in the sandy desert is a great exercise, but after the first couple of miles it ceases to be fun.

Now here was J. W. Black with a device that bid fair to revolutionize the whole problem of desert exploration.

The boys cranked up a machine for me to try. I was smart enough to tackle a medium slope first because I had never ridden a motorcycle in my life and the small amount of time I had put in on a bicycle had been many, many years ago.

I soon made a series of astounding discoveries.

Where Black, who is tall, long-legged and heavily muscled, could ride with the greatest of ease, I couldn't go at all.

Where Sam Hicks, who is tall, strong, long-legged and with the good sense of balance which comes to a bronc-stomper, could get by very handily, I was stymied.

I am short-legged, chunky and, while I argue with myself about it from time to time, I have to admit that I am no longer quite as young as I used to be.

In order to get top performance in those original models J. W. Black had to incorporate quite a bit of weight. They weighed around a hundred and seventy-five pounds. When a machine would start to tip over, a long-legged man could put his foot down on the ground and straighten it up. By the time a short-legged man got his foot to the ground the machine had moved over far enough from its center of gravity so that all the weight seemed to be directly over that reaching foot, and on ground which sloped away steeply the results could be disastrous.

In my case they were painful in the extreme.

I became afraid I might sprain an ankle or seriously injure myself in these practice runs; and that was unthinkable. If I was going to bust up, I wanted it to be while I was on an adventure. And I couldn't bear the thought of an injury that would keep me from starting out on the trip.

After all, I assured myself, once I got out in the desert I would pick up the knack of the thing very quickly.

So we got everything all ready for an early morning start. We sat up that night building air castles and I was too excited to sleep.

The next morning long before daylight we were up and away.

That day turned out to be the beginning of desert summer, when the weather changed.

Usually in the Southern California desert, sometime in May the season changes overnight from a cool spring to a boiling hot summer, and of course that was the time we picked for our desert exploration.

We had four-wheel-drive vehicles and we took them out in the desert until we reached a spot where we could establish a base camp and unload our Pak-Jaks.

Out there in the scorching sun the heat was simply terrific. We parked two of the pickups parallel at a distance of about fifteen feet apart and stretched canvas between them, thereby making an impromptu shade. Prudence dictated that we spend the hot part of the day in the shade and go out around four or five o'clock in the afternoon to do our exploring.

But Black couldn't wait to try out his invention and he

The Pak-Jak is designed for exploring rough country.

cranked up and took off. Sam followed him, and I came limping along behind.

It was then I realized that I had a whole lot to learn about riding scooters.

This was rough terrain. There was a trail of sorts. There were deep gullies, steep banks, rocks and, above all, there were the spines of cactus— beaver-tail cactus, prickly pear cactus, cholla cactus, biznaga cactus — all with spines; long, hard, penetrating spines.

To the uninitiated, riding a motor scooter which goes no faster than fifteen miles an hour may seem simple, but the throttle is located in the grip of the right handlebar. If you move your wrist away from you, you shut the motor down. If you move it toward you, you open the motor, and the entire difference between idling speed and full throttle is only an inch or so of turning space.

As I subsequently discovered, whenever I got in a tight place my instinctive reactions would be dead wrong. I would open the contraption to full speed when I was trying to slow down. I also found that I had bike rider's hypnosis.

If I were skirting a barranca with a big rock in the bottom I would say to myself, "Now, no matter what happens I must keep out of that barranca, and at all costs avoid that big rock — that big rock — that big rock."

I'd then find myself heading straight toward the barranca and the rock. I would try to slow down and instead would open the machine wide open. It would give a snort, rear up on its hind legs, so to speak, then come down to a level and make a roaring dash down the slope, bang against the rock.

I would fly through the air with the greatest of ease.

As I have mentioned, I have arrived at an age when my bones are supposed to be brittle, but I disproved that theory. I came down in a series of somersaults. I lit on my hip, I lit on my shoulder, I lit on my head and on my belly. I slid over granite rocks. I hit boulders, I scraped skin, I bruised knees but I broke no bones.

Gradually I began to get enough of the hang of it so I could ride a somewhat wobbling course in the general direction I wanted to go, and speedily the scorching sunlight (we learned afterwards it was a hundred and seventeen in the deep shade at the nearest desert watering station), ran up my blood pressure and made me more and more uncomfortable.

I finally zigzagged my way back to camp and, grabbing a canteen, drank copious quantities of sun-heated water, taste-tainted by the metallic container from which it had come. Nevertheless, that warm drink with the flavor of galvanized iron was sweet nectar to my parched throat.

I rested for an hour, put peroxide on my scraped skin, bandaged up the places where I was bleeding, and tried to relax.

It was just too darned hot to relax, and I was bruised and smarting and sore.

Up on the mountains to the north of us I could hear occasionally the put-put-put of a motor as one of the others opened up his throttle and occasionally I could see a little black speck inching along up the slopes.

It was too much for me. I tried it again.

I had more of the same experience. I came back and rested and then tried it for the third time. The fascination of those machines is irresistible.

About the time it began to cool off, when we should have been trying out the vehicles, the others came back to camp. They were enthusiastic, overheated and nearly exhausted.

We decided we'd get to a cooler place. There was some desert mountain country we wanted to explore, where there were caves and shade and huge piles of granite at an elevation of some three thousand feet. It should be cooler up there.

So we loaded up the machines and started fighting our way along sandy back roads which consisted of little more than two tracks in the deep sand. However, by the time darkness overtook us we were fairly close to one of the main highways and knew that we could get into the granite country the next morning before it got too terribly hot.

That night there was a full moon.

Various atmospheric conditions change the *apparent* size of the moon. I don't know why this is true, but it is an optical fact, although a scientist with proper instruments could undoubtedly demonstrate that it is only an illusion.

In any event, on that night, which was hot and still, the moon seemed as big as a balloon and the desert was bathed with soft moonlight which turned the sand to silver.

We were camped in a section of the desert where there was a good deal of vegetation, quite a bit of greasewood, sagebrush, saltbush, cholla cactus, an occasional verde tree, and smoke trees.

There was not the faintest breath of air stirring.

We usually go to bed early on camping trips, partly because

we like to get up early and partly because there is nothing else to do. With the dishes out of the way after supper, we sit around the campfire for a little while and then go to bed, wearied by a day which has been packed with excitement.

On this night, however, it was too hot for a campfire, even for sociable purposes. We had done our cooking on a gasoline stove and we sat around for a little while, then spread out our sleeping bags.

It was too hot to get inside a sleeping bag. I opened my bag up and lay there with nothing over me. My upper side was not too warm, but the side that was down on the sleeping bag became hot, so I would turn over from time to time. I noticed that the others were doing the same.

It was difficult to get to sleep early that night.

Then I heard the sound of a motor and looked up.

J. W. Black had started his Pak-Jak and was wending his way out through the desert, following animal trails which twisted and skirted along the edges of barrancas, avoiding the sharp spines of the cactus.

Sam followed suit, and then I couldn't resist the temptation.

I got my tortured body up off the sleeping bag, and attired in pajamas and slippers, started my motor and eased my way out into the desert.

That was one of the most wonderful experiences I have ever had.

The air was warm when one stayed in one place, but on the Pak-Jaks, the man-made current fanned all parts of the body. A speed of eight or ten miles an hour can create quite a cooling breeze.

The moonlight was bright enough so that one could have read a newspaper, at least the smaller headlines. The moon was still in the east so that the foliage cast long pools of dark shadow, deepening the mystery of the spell cast by the desert.

I had painfully acquired a certain degree of skill so that I was now able to pilot the Pak-Jak more or less instinctively and seldom made the mistake of opening the throttle wide open when I wanted to close it.

On the other hand, the natural handicaps of the desert made piloting a Pak-Jak a somewhat hazardous experience. It was necessary to pick out the right trails and on one occasion I came to grief when the trail I was following ran out to skirt the very edge of a sand wash some six or eight feet deep.

The animals who had made that trail, probably coyotes and foxes, could patter along the edge of the wash without any trouble. But when it came to carrying the weight of the hundred-and-seventy-five-pound Pak-Jak and a hundred-and-seventy-five-pound rider, the sand simply wouldn't take it. However, I didn't dare detour from the trail because of a collection of cholla cacti on the left. So I got as far away from the edge as possible and started to slow my throttle.

The whole edge of the little barranca caved in and I found myself riding a miniature avalanche down to the bottom. Strangely enough, I managed to turn the wheel at just the right time and in just the right way so I kept upright, and went sailing up the bottom of the sandy wash looking for an opportunity to get back to the level on which I had been cruising.

I finally found a place where I could open the throttle, charge into the bank and, after a suspenseful moment, emerge on top, where I found a trail and was once more on my way.

That riding was so exciting, so absolutely perfect that no one wanted to quit and go to bed. I rode for about an hour and then reluctantly came in and parked my machine, started to get down on my sleeping bag, heard the others riding out in the desert, cranked up again and went out and rode for another hour or two.

By the time we came back the night had cooled considerably and we sank into exhausted but restful slumber. Along toward morning it even became so cool a very light blanket was acceptable.

The next morning we were up with the first streaks of dawn and had breakfast. It was almost cool enough to be comfortable.

We headed back toward the nearest paved highway. By nine o'clock we were at the ghost city of Tubac.

Here and there the desert is dotted with ghost towns. Some of them are famous. Some of them are towns that died a natural death under such circumstances that even the corpses seem to be unimportant.

The latter are the ones that I like.

The more famous ghost towns have been written up and then rewritten, photographed, and rephotographed. In some

Calico, one of the famous ghost towns, has been "restored" and has become quite a tourist attraction.

places there are *no trespassing* signs and from nearby towns one can buy colored post cards. But towns like Tubac expired unnoticed and then the bones bleached in the sun, a town too isolated for even the souvenir hunters to vandalize.

Stores once thriving with business are now boxes of bleached boards. *The* big house on the hill which dominated all the social and economic activities of the town still remains somewhat aloof, slightly disdainful even in death.

And all around are various odds and ends of junk, souvenirs of bygone days.

We went on from Tubac and as the day warmed up, reached the main highway from San Bernardino to Needles.

It seemed considerably cooler than the day before, but when we stopped for gasoline we noticed a thermometer tucked away in the deep shade underneath a double roof—the thermometer read a hundred and seventeen.

We traveled a few miles, then left the paved highway and started toward the granite country, climbing up to an elevation of over three thousand feet and emerging from the stifling blanket of heat which had settled over the desert.

We made camp at the mouth of one of the caves. Within a few minutes we had our Pak-Jaks out and had started exploring.

This was a new type of travel, even more exciting. We were able to work our way among granite upthrusts, over wind-worn, rocky ledges down into dry stream beds and into an ever-new country.

Some of the caves apparently had never been explored because we found several Indian metates still in place, just as they had been left by the long dead occupants.

We didn't disturb those metates, although they are greatly prized as relics and souvenirs by many a desert traveler.

We thought they looked better where they were than in someone's patio, and we received such a thrill from entering

J. W. Black (with beard) and Sam Hicks explore the granite country on Pak-Jaks.

a cave knowing that no souvenir hunters had been there before us, that we wanted to leave it as we found it.

Sometime later I wrote up the trip in a magazine and illustrated the article with photographs. Some of the smart readers, recognizing the contours of some of the mountains, managed to find where we had been camped and retraced our steps. A short time ago when I returned to show some companions caves that had never been looted, we found all the metates had been taken and all the dirt removed from the floors of the cave and sifted for Indian arrowheads and other souvenirs.

Such is life.

The weather continued cool up there in the mountains, at least reasonably cool, but the desert and the lowlands were wrapped in a heat blanket.

Only 117° in the Shade—But No Shade!

We had with us an all-band battery-powered radio and from time to time we got weather reports telling of sweltering heat, and, in the municipal areas, heavy smog.

Up where we were in the granite peaks the air was crystal clear and when we felt like it we could crawl into some little cave, stretch out and watch the wildlife – rabbits, quail, doves, and on one occasion, a coyote.

Theoretically we had committed ourselves to do some exploring on the Peg-Leg Smith Mine in the vicinity of the Chocolate Mountains, but the temptation of the present was too great and we rode our Pak-Jaks on trips of long exploration around through the granite.

J. W., true to the form of inventors everywhere, jotted down ideas for improvements he could make. It was astonishing how many of them he thought up and how practical they turned out to be. Looking back on it, those early models of the Pak-Jaks were crude, awkward and unwieldy, as compared with the models we are now riding.

But they were a revelation to us. They not only opened up a new form of adventure, but were wonderful exercise and a source of great pleasure.

Gradually I was learning something about controlling the contraption, but it was a slow and painful process. I took one beautiful spill down the face of a granite slide and my right arm was skinned from the wrist to near the shoulder. By the time we were ready to head for home I was a mass of bandages, scraped skin and soreness, but we had had fun.

However, we determined that our survey of the famous lost mines of the desert would be postponed until fall when the weather became cooler. A hundred and seventeen in the shade is hot, but when there is no shade it is terrific.

It was in this granite country that we had a nightly serenade by the coyotes, a sound that only the camper in the wilds can enjoy to the fullest.

Chapter Seven
An Intimate Look at the Coyote

I have never yet heard anything which approximates the chilling sound of a coyote's call. It will start with a shrill, high-pitched, rapid yap-yap-yap. Then the yappings will become more rapid, more shrill, and somewhere, somehow the coyote manages to get an overtone built into the sound itself so that the listener could swear there were two or three animals involved in the cacophony.

The sound swells in volume and is a cross between a combined yapping and a long-drawn wail, only the two seem to overlap.

Apparently there *are* times when other coyotes will chime in and then it seems that there are a dozen animals engaged in a crescendo of salutation to the moon and the stars.

Sometimes there are no preliminary yap-yap-yap barks but the coyote plunges at once into a full-fledged screaming wail.

Highly strung individuals seated around a campfire are inclined to jump instinctively at the sound of the coyote's scream, and even the old-timers require a hundredth of a second or so to become adjusted.

One thing I have against the television programs depicting life in the "Wild West" is the fact that when the camp is made and the firelight is flickering on the faces of the well-made-up heroes someone always tries to make the surroundings convincing by bringing in the sound of a coyote.

Hollywood's idea of what a coyote sounds like is apparently what the creative minds think a coyote *should* sound like, and if he doesn't really sound that way it's just too bad. The coyote had better watch a few pictures on the television screen and change his howling.

For some reason I like Western shows, but the things that an audience is asked to put up with are almost beyond human endurance.

The hero is called upon to escort some delicate morsel of femininity from San Francisco to Reno. The camera shows them starting out and galloping bravely across the desert, with the snow-capped mountains in the background.

Where anyone would find a long desert stretch with snow-capped mountains in the background between San Francisco and Reno is not clear, but there they are. Hollywood has simply moved the Mojave Desert four hundred miles farther north and you can like it or leave it.

Then comes the night and the campfire. From some mysterious source blankets have been produced. There is a huge frying pan and an oversized coffeepot, one that would hold enough coffee for a dozen cowpunchers. Apparently the audience is not supposed to overlook the fact that the heroes are camping out.

Then comes the howl of a coyote, obviously a recording made by some animal imitator who reasons that a coyote is a wild dog and therefore the noise should be something like the barking of a dog, only different.

Then the firelight flickers out and, after a commercial, comes the dawn of the new day with the hero cooking bacon and eggs in the frying pan and the coffeepot bubbling merrily away.

Now, I submit that riding horseback from San Francisco to Reno without a pack horse would be quite an undertaking. Carrying blankets and provisions on a saddle horse is a major problem, and some of the oversized coffeepots that I have seen on Western television shows would almost require a two-wheel trailer.

At about this time the script calls for the villain to start shooting. Bullets strike the rocks around the makeshift fireplace, glancing off with the screaming ricochet heard so frequently in television. Three bullets hit the coffeepot and knock it helter-skelter, and four or five bullets hit the fire and send embers flying.

The hero rolls behind a rock for protection, draws his six-gun and opens a fusillade. The heroine is crouched down behind the rock where she has modestly spent the night.

Big as that coffeepot is, it requires pretty good marksmanship to hit it three or four times in succession. That is, it should be possible to kill the hero by hitting him with at least one coffeepot shot.

It is not clear whether the desperado is shooting at the hero and missing him and hitting the coffeepot, or whether the coffeepot is the target, the theory being that if he can get rid of the coffeepot the hero won't be able to last in the desert.

The mortality of Hollywood coffeepots must be tremendous.

The battle progresses. It would have taken two pack horses to carry the ammunition that is expended. The hero jumps up from behind the rock and snaps off a shot, then ducks, and just as he ducks a bullet hits the rock and screams off into the distance.

Again the hero raises his head, shoots and ducks, and again bullets hit the rock and ricochet.

However, I really don't care if the hero would have had to start out with his pockets bulging with ammunition, the coffeepot slung over his back, carrying a dozen eggs in the bandana wrapped around his neck, and bacon in a chamois-skin money belt, if they would only make the coyote sound less synthetic.

Perhaps if they ever did get a tape recording of an actual coyote in full cry, half the audience wouldn't believe it was real and the other half would be scared to death.

In one of my northern hideouts I was troubled with a particularly persistent coyote who was apparently trying to lure my dogs out into the night. It may have been a female with amorous tendencies, or it may have been a single coyote belonging to a pack lying in ambush nearby ready to jump a dog as soon as it came out. In either event, the facts of canine biology being what they are, the experience would have been fatal for a dog. Even if the female coyote had been in good faith and her intentions had been honorable, the probabilities are that the dog would have been torn limb from limb by his potential rivals.

Fortunately my dogs were sufficiently sophisticated by ranch life and instinct to recognize the danger, and when the coyote called they seemed to shrink within their skins and lie closer to the floor.

The "come-on" call of the coyote is essentially different from the full-throated cry one hears when the coyotes are having a social gathering, or when one of them wishes to broadcast to the stars and the moon. It is a series of rapid, high-pitched yelps, starting abruptly and stopping abruptly.

One night in particular a coyote was especially persistent. Because I need a lot of elbow room in my work I have a study built next to my house trailer and there is a sleeping porch on the study. Sometimes I sleep in the adjoining house trailer, sometimes on the sleeping porch. On the night in question, I was on the sleeping porch, which was within ten or fifteen yards of a manzanita thicket which covered several acres.

The coyote approached apparently to the edge of the manzanita thicket.

I jumped up and turned a powerful flashlight into the thicket.

The coyote was too smart to look at the flashlight and let me see the glint of his eyes. The barking ceased abruptly. There was silence, and the beam of the flashlight illuminated only the twisted trunks and branches of the big manzanita bushes.

I decided I had eliminated the disturbance for the evening, shut off the light and went back to bed.

No sooner had my body hit the bed than the coyote, apparently still in his original position, started his yap-yap . . . yap-yap-yap . . . yap-yap.

In this particular camp our bedrooms are in house trailers scattered around through the acreage so that each person can have on whatever radio program he wants without interfering with the others, or can sit up as late at night as he cares to without a light shining into someone's eyes.

I thought of shooting off a gun but decided it would waken too many people who would want explanations. I put off shouting as long as I could for fear of disturbing others, but as the coyote continued for some ten or fifteen minutes I finally got up with a flashlight and shouted.

Once again the beam of the flashlight exposed only manzanita. Once again there was silence.

Again I got back to bed and the minute I did the coyote, apparently still in the same position, started the same old song of enticement.

The dogs were watching me with condescending amusement.

Suddenly I got the right idea.

I hooked up a tape recorder, pointed the microphone toward the manzanita thicket and waited.

I had about five minutes to wait, then the coyote started in with the same old yap-yap-yapping.

I let him yap for about a minute and a half, then wound the recorded tape back on the spool, raised the volume of the machine to its highest level, plugged in an extension speaker which I put out near the thicket, and got back into bed.

The coyote was a little suspicious of what I had been doing and it was about ten minutes before the yap-yap-yapping started.

I instantly thumbed the switch which started the tape recorder playing.

From the extension speaker out in the darkness came a perfect reproduction of the coyote's voice.

That did it.

Not only was there silence for the rest of the evening but I have never heard that coyote again. Yet prior to this time he had been a regular visitor and had given us a nightly "come-on."

I have often wondered what the coyote thought when the amplified sound came yapping back at him from the extension speaker. Whatever it was, it achieved the desired effect. That was over a year ago and the coyote has never returned.

We had a tame coyote at one time; that is, he was a wild-tame coyote.

We found him as a pup, suffering from either distemper or pneumonia. He could hardly breathe. We put him under a warm stove and nursed him back to health.

He would never tolerate a cage. I lived in my study and the coyote lived there with me. I put in a box of sand and the coyote recognized this as a home and not a cage.

As he grew up we learned things about coyotes that we would never have learned otherwise.

Bravo in a strawberry patch.

The coyote's sense of direction was absolutely uncanny.

While he was just a little shaver about the size of two fists I would take him for a walk with the dogs, holding him in my arms and letting him watch the dogs as they ran along the trails, darting into the sagebrush patches, occasionally flushing a rabbit which they would pursue gleefully with shrill yelps of excitement.

The coyote never made any effort to break away to follow but would snuggle in my arms watching everything that went on with eyes that never missed a thing.

Eventually we would turn back toward my study.

The coyote would promptly proceed to growl ominously as though he were about to sink his teeth into my arm.

Not wanting him to grow up to be vicious, I would cuff his ears and speak sharply to him.

At those times he seemed to feel that his last friend on earth had turned against him.

I subsequently found out that those low throaty growls were not a prelude to viciousness or an attack of any sort. They were simply the coyote's means of expressing himself, a variety of coyote talk. He would wag his tail when he was pleased and growl when he was displeased. One meant yes, one meant no.

So then I tried to test the coyote by walking in a circle which would gradually bring me back to my study.

As long as the circle was headed slightly away from the study, the coyote was happy. The minute it started even slightly back toward the study, the coyote started growling.

After the coyote got his growth I found that it was possible to start him yapping by giving a single off-key whistle or making some shrill noise.

I think that the yapping in response to my whistle was probably his way of answering me.

By that time, we had turned him loose to go out and fend for himself. He lived in the brush in the hills back of the ranch, and whenever I gave this shrill off-key whistle he would answer with a couple of yaps. If I then imitated a coyote barking, he would be very likely to answer me with a series of barks, and if I kept calling he would come down out of the brush to see what it was I wanted, standing there looking at me in a puzzled manner as if to say, "Well, what is it? What's it all about?"

Apparently I had used coyote talk he could understand, but I failed to appreciate the significance of what I had said. It was as though I had said, "Come on down, you're wanted on the telephone," and then when he got down and found that I was nowhere near the telephone and that no one wanted him, he would be puzzled.

I could write a whole book about the antics of this coyote and the things he taught us.

I would take him out to an isolated part of the ranch,

A tussle with Jean.

raise my voice in an imitation of a coyote bark, and he would promptly join in. Once he started howling it seemed that he couldn't quit until he had had his howl out.

At such times he would squat on his haunches, elevate his muzzle, and sound would pour from his throat with such rapidity that one could hardly distinguish the separate barks which were component parts of his howling wail.

The coyote is a loyal friend, a daring adversary.

As far as the sheepmen are concerned, the coyote is a menace. Poultry raisers who live in isolated communities where the poultry can run out, also regard the coyote with an unfriendly eye. For the rest, however, the coyote is an interesting part of the scenery, a picturesque dash of local color.

Contrary to much that has been written, the big cattlemen whom I know regard the coyote as a friend. He keeps down the rodents which tunnel into irrigation ditches, he keeps down the mice population, and on the whole he does a lot more good than harm.

To the coyote, man is a fiend incarnate.

The things that men do to coyotes are horrible, and if they were generally known the human race would hide its head in shame and popular clamor would demand that the practices be discontinued.

Yet, in spite of all the scientific methods of extermination waged against him, the coyote continues to exist. It is a precarious existence. The coyotes never live to a ripe old age. They have been threatened with extinction in certain communities, but somehow enough of them survive to keep the species alive.

The average citizen fails to realize that a portion of his tax money is used for cruelties which beggar description.

It has been said our government is one of checks and balances. It might also be said that our government is one of organized minorities and pressure groups.

Using the sheepmen as a stalking horse behind which to hide, people who want to upset the balance of nature and politicians who want patronage in the form of jobs to be given, have organized various high-sounding names such as, "Predator Control," etc.

Actually, a substantial part of this program does a little good and a lot of harm. It wages a war of extermination upon animals, many of whom are more beneficial than otherwise, and it utilizes the latest developments of science to perpetrate diabolical cruelties on the coyote.

The coyote is readily adaptable. He is quick to learn. He is shrewd. He is constantly alert and, as animals go, he has a great fund of ingenuity. He is mischievous, daring, and he has a highly developed sense of humor. It is my own opinion that a coyote can think circles around any dog I ever saw.

When men introduced steel traps the coyotes quickly learned all about them. Men buried steel traps in the dust along trails used by the coyotes. The steel was rubbed with bacon rind so that it would have no trace of human scent. But the coyotes learned to dig up the steel traps, spring them, and go on their way.

Then science entered the picture – science and the taxpayer's money.

It takes a long while to eradicate an instinct that is bred into one. This is true of man and it is doubly true of animals.

Start a crackling fire at night in the open and tell a man not to go near it. If there is a really powerful reason why he shouldn't go near it, a man can keep away from it, but otherwise he will go stand in front of the fire, toasting his front and then his back, or, if it is a small fire, extend his open hands over the coals in order to feel the welcome warmth.

A coyote wants to live. The rules of life in the raw are not gentle. In order to live, a coyote must protect his range against the encroachment of others.

Perhaps the strongest instinct of all is that calling for the perpetuation of the species. Man cannot resist the mating call and neither can the coyote.

With the coyote, communication is largely by scent. He has a delicate sense of smell which is beyond human comprehension.

Man, who has no longer any need for a sense of smell, retains only a rudimentary ability to detect odors which would be overpowering to an animal.

This is because man is able to communicate by voice.

The coyote, not having the power to communicate anywhere near as well as man does by means of his vocal cords, relies upon the sense of smell.

We see the same thing in dogs.

One dog meeting another will smell him all over and as a

result of that appraisal learn a lot about him; where the other came from, what kind of a home he has, what sort of food he is eating, and much about his past history.

Until a male has once mated he is virtually immune from attack as far as other dogs are concerned, but after he has once taken a female to mate the others know this instantly and will take him on in combat.

Dogs have certain property rights which they mark by scent. The average dog is willing to respect the property rights of another except when a more belligerent dog leaves his scent on top of the other's.

When those two dogs meet they're going to fight. The gauntlet has been hurled. One of them has to be master.

That is the reason that sometimes neighbors express surprise when their dogs which are otherwise remarkably well-behaved, suddenly and without warning lunge into deadly combat.

All these actions and reactions are natural instincts which are a part of an animal's life.

Coyotes mark their "range." Coyotes detecting the odor of a female that is willing to receive their attentions, lose their sense of prudence just as some Sugar Daddy will lose all perspective upon being exposed to the blandishments of a curvaceous gold digger.

Thus scientists, finding the different scents which appeal to the coyote and carefully analyzing them, have been able to produce synthetic substitutes which arouse instincts in the coyote more powerful than reason.

A tuft of cotton in the midst of a trail followed by coyotes emits an odor so tantalizing that the coyote's instincts cause him to lick the cotton with his tongue, to pull at it gently. This cotton, upon being disturbed, triggers a mechanism buried in the ground which, in turn, releases a charge of deadly cyanic gas into the mouth and nostrils of the coyote.

Sam Hicks is in a position to know something of how a coyote feels under these circumstances.

Sam had lived for a long time in the wilds of Wyoming. He has the eye of a mountaineer and the instincts of a hunter.

Once when these scientific lethal weapons had first been perfected, Sam saw a peculiar tuft the size of his thumb in a faint game trail he was following. He stooped to pick it up with thumb and forefinger, and received a charge of cyanic gas right in the face.

People whose selfish interests are served by having a goodly share of taxpayers' money go to support poisoners, trappers and professional destroyers of wildlife, have insisted that there isn't enough cyanide in one of the deadly contraptions to kill a man.

Apparently they are right.

Sam didn't die.

He staggered off to the side of the trail, gasping for breath and thinking he was going to die. After a while the effects wore off, but it was a harrowing experience and he had a taste of how the coyote must feel.

I myself had at one time mute evidence of how a coyote feels about one of these machines.

I found the discharged metallic gas cartridge on the ground, and despite the fact it was made of metal it had been flattened and dented by the jaws of a coyote, with tooth marks visible all over it.

Some coyote had felt a sufficient fury toward this man-made destructive device to sink his teeth into the hard metal again and again and again, and then discard it.

It couldn't have been the coyote who sprung the trap because that coyote was dead. It must have been the coyote's mate.

While there is some argument about it, apparently coyotes mate for life.

A shotgun shell literally chewed to pieces by resentful coyotes.

One can imagine the feelings of a coyote moving silently along through the night, happy, with his mate at his side, searching for game that would perhaps support a litter of pups at home. Then suddenly the mate touches a tuft of cotton. There is an explosion. The mate, gasping for breath, staggers to the side of the trail and after a few agonizing moments, expires.

The surviving coyote digs up the offending instrument of death with his forepaws and vents his vengeance upon it.

I have seen the same things done with gun cartridges, and since I have learned what to look for, find that quite often the various paraphernalia associated with man's means of scientific destruction are set upon by a coyote in what is apparently a frenzy of rage.

After I started this book I wanted to photograph some of these cartridges but I had mislaid the ones I had saved and couldn't locate them. So Sam Hicks and David Hurtado discharged a few shotgun shells and threw the empty casings away in a grape vineyard which was frequented by coyotes.

The next morning they went out and found a cartridge which had literally been chewed to pieces by a visiting coyote, one who evidently had had experience with man's ingenious methods of destruction.

Of course these mechanical methods of animal destruction are crude compared with the subtle way of poison.

Scientists are now inventing a variety of poisons, each deadlier than its predecessor, each designed to exterminate a certain type of wildlife, each so deadly that it is unbelievably successful, not only for the purpose for which it was designed, but also through chain reaction, in destroying much of life that is necessary to man.

Much of this has been exposed in the book, *Silent Spring*, by Rachel Carson.

The ground squirrel in the southwest is one of the most persistent procreators of all time. Against him man has devised poisons of such ingenuity and power that it seems impossible that any ground squirrel could survive.

Each year poisoned grain is put temptingly down the holes of the ground squirrel. The theory is that the ground squirrels alone will eat this poisoned grain, draw back in their holes and die.

Actually thousands of ground squirrels die in the open and the hungry coyote in search of a meal, finding the tempting ground squirrel stretched out in death with the body still warm, gorges himself after the fashion of wild carnivore everywhere, only to find that he himself has absorbed the poison.

There are times around my ranch when the coyote population increases to the extent that we can hear them almost every night, sometimes several times during a night. Then comes the biological survey with its spreading poison and all of a sudden the nights are silent.

The silence of death.

Chapter Eight
Two Veteran Desert Characters

Much of my recent desert exploration has been by helicopter. Using this aircraft to explore unknown terrain gives one a picture which can be obtained by no other means. But it takes time to arrange for helicopters and get them on the job.

I have been particularly fortunate in that the Hiller Aircraft Corporation comes out with a new model just about as often as I come up with a new idea for adventure. The company likes to demonstrate what these new models will do under rough conditions, and I am the man to furnish the rough conditions.

Their latest model is so designed that vibration is reduced to a minimum. It is particularly adapted for survey reconnaissance and there are other improvements which are technical and which therefore mean a lot to them but just don't mean a darned thing to me. However, knowing of his new model, I got in touch with Bob Boughton on the phone and told him enough about the Lost Arch Mine and the Lost Dutch Oven Mine to arouse his interest.

I pointed out that by exploring the Turtle Mountains with

helicopters we could almost certainly locate the site of the arch — unless it had been destroyed by earthquake. The only question in my mind was whether we could locate it within the time allotted for exploration.

Then again, in the Clipper Mountains, the Lost Dutch Oven Mine was marked by certain physical landmarks which Schoefield had described, a wide trail running from a spring up to the mining camp, and two portals so close that one could only squeeze through with a pack burro.

Schoefield at the time of his discovery had been working for the Santa Fe Railroad and was residing at the location of the tunnel they were putting through from the Clipper Mountains to Danby.

We knew from experience that once a trail has been marked in the hard desert country where it is away from blowing sand the marks of that trail will last for many years. At times we have followed trails that were well over two hundred years old.

Jack Hicks explores an ancient, wide trail.

The author and Bob Boughton inspect one of the helicopters.

We felt certain that we could find physical clues by the aid of a helicopter which would enable us to relocate the sites of both these lost mines.

Our income tax laws being what they are, I don't know what I'd do with one of the things if I found it, but it's fascinating to look for the pot of gold at the end of the rainbow.

I found Bob Boughton in a receptive mood. The idea of hunting for lost mines interested him, the idea of demonstrating the new model helicopter in the rough mountainous regions of the desert sounded very attractive. So we started lining up our calendars.

As part of our program of exploration, I decided to get in touch with the Wilhelm brothers and see what they were doing.

The Wilhelm brothers are two of the most colorful characters I have ever known, and they know the desert the way a sophisticated city dweller knows the streets and avenues, the shops and restaurants of his town.

Bob Boughton.

Walt Wilhelm, the author, and Ken Wilhelm thirty years ago.

Walt Wilhelm has been interested in primitive weapons for just about all his life. Ken Wilhelm, the younger brother, is interested in any idea provided it is wild enough.

Thirty years ago, when I was doing quite a bit of shooting with the bow and arrow, the Wilhelm brothers were without exception the most remarkable trick shots in the world — at least I have never seen many of their feats duplicated and have never heard of anyone willing to try them.

Walt Wilhelm used a blowgun as well as a bow and arrow and became very expert with it. He experimented with different metals, different diameters, and different types of blowgun projectiles until he had reached a maximum efficiency with velocity and impact.

As far as bow and arrow shooting was concerned they began where others left off.

One of the brothers thought nothing of shooting an apple off the other brother's head, using a heavy bow and an arrow

Walt Wilhelm, the author and Ken Wilhelm thirty years ago.

that would have cracked the human skull like an eggshell — in fact one of their stunts was to take a frying pan and blast the bottom out of it with an arrow, going clean through the metal.

But in the course of time shooting an apple became too tame. They started shooting ping-pong balls, match boxes and, finally, at the request of a motion picture operator who wanted to film the stunt, Ken Wilhelm shot a cuff button off Walt Wilhelm's head.

In those days the brothers had a car which they called "The Prowler." The Prowler was Walt Wilhelm's pride and joy. He had designed it with loving care.

This was long before the day of the four-wheel-drive automobile. It was before balloon tires, when hard, high-pressure tires would spin in sand, dig their way in and leave the motorist hopelessly stranded.

I am not enough of a mechanic to pretend to know what

was done or how it was done, but Walt worked out some scheme of putting transmissions back to back and finally wound up with a car that wouldn't go faster than fifteen miles an hour with the motor wide open, but would go so slowly that the wheels were barely turning. Then he took huge cast-off truck tires, put them on oversized wheels, stripped the automobile down to bare essentials, and he and Ken would start out in the desert, literally going anywhere they pleased.

They negotiated sidehills so steep that they rolled the car over several times but they were both young and active and they jumped clear and regarded the incident as great sport. Twice they turned the car end over end, jumped clear, righted the car and went on.

I remember one time when they took me around a sidehill so steep that the car begin to slide sideways. At that point I shamelessly bailed out, running down that sidehill just as fast as I could run.

When I looked back I found that my cameras had also spilled out and they, too, were rolling down the hill.

The brothers armored the bottom of the car so that when they came to the edge of a desert wash, they could roll the front wheels over; then, when the body of the car struck the edge of the wash, it would start a little avalanche which they could ride down to the bottom. Whenever they wanted to go anywhere in the desert they simply headed in a general direction and off they went.

They discovered things that no one else had ever even heard of. Among other things they found the scene of a battle between cavalrymen and Indians, with bones, tarnished brass buttons, decayed saddles and the remnants of arrows.

They had always wanted to take me on what they called a real trip, but in those days, with very limited time at my disposal and a greater degree of prudence than that possessed by either of the brothers, I made only short trips in

The Prowler. Those trips furnished me with all the excitement I needed.

In those days the brothers were free-lancing. They would start out on some foolhardy expedition and make it pay off one way or another. Walt became a pretty good photographer, got a typewriter and sold a few articles here and there.

Together they made several motion pictures of shooting stunts with blowguns and bows and arrows, and of The Prowler in places no one would ever believe a wheeled vehicle could negotiate.

The plots of these motion pictures, if they could be called plots, were wild in the extreme. They were made up from time to time and place to place as the photographer and producer tried to think up things that would shock an audience.

No matter how wild the stunts became, the brothers "went along with the gag," as the saying goes. They weren't going to be the ones to chicken out and the picture people took full advantage of their attitude.

The things that were thought up and the things that were done are almost unbelievable. Most of the people who saw these pictures thought they were faked. I happen to know they were absolutely genuine. Everything that appeared to be done was actually done just as it was shown. There was no faking.

In one motion picture the creative minds decided it would be a wonderful idea if the brothers would pursue a wildcat up a mountain trail, flanked by a sheer wall so that the wildcat couldn't get off it, which would come to a dead end at a cave in which the bobcat was to take refuge.

The brothers would be equipped with a homemade net fashioned out of soft yarn, and Ken Wilhelm would climb along this narrow trail, which furnished only precarious footing, until he came to the mouth of the cave, holding the net in his left hand and spreading it with the tip of his bow which would be held in his right hand.

Theoretically, at this time the bobcat would oblige by coming out and getting tangled up in the net.

In the meantime, a huge rattlesnake would have moved in behind Ken so that Ken would have a raging wildcat in a soft net on his hands in front and a huge rattlesnake ready to strike just behind him.

At this critical moment Walt, some twenty or thirty feet behind, would raise his blowgun and dispose of the snake with a dart.

The brothers knew of a very steep bluff along the side of a dry wash where there was a game trail some six or eight inches wide, terminating in a cave which had evidently been a coyote den. The face of the cliff was so abrupt that even an enraged bobcat couldn't get up it. There would be only one way for the bobcat to come back and that was down the trail.

Another shot of The Prowler in action.

The brothers also knew where they could find a particularly mean, vicious wildcat which had been trapped, which strenuously objected to a short life of captivity, and which tried to chew up everybody who came close to the cage.

They prowled around until they found a rattlesnake. The script called for a rattlesnake six feet long, but they weren't quite able to make it. They got one about five feet long.

The caged wildcat was taken to the trail and released. He promptly started running up the trail, along the perpendicular bluff and into the cave. He then found there was no place else for him to go.

Ken took the trail in pursuit and at the proper time Walt threw him the homemade net.

Then the enraged rattlesnake was planted on the trail and he in turn had no place to go.

The stage was set.

The actors brought themselves on.

The bobcat, finding that he was trapped at the end of a trail and knowing that Ken was on his way up, decided there was no reason for him to wait in the cave until the script called for him to emerge. Since he didn't like life in a cage, he decided the best thing for him to do was to dispose of Ken and Walter Wilhelm by a counterattack.

So the huge bobcat came out onto the trail launching an offensive, and Ken, trying to juggle the net, gave a little ground.

The enraged rattlesnake warned Ken to keep his distance.

At this point the script called for a head shot on the snake to be made by Walt Wilhelm.

The distance, however, was thirty or forty feet, the snake was moving and writhing, and Walt's first dart hit the snake in the body, serving only to convince him that the enemy in front should be eliminated.

At that moment the wildcat made his purposeful charge and Ken, throwing the net over him, found that it was somewhat inadequate.

Walt's second shot was a bull's eye. He struck the snake directly in the head, pinning his jaws with the dart and killing him instantly.

The dead snake slithered down the perpendicular side of the barranca.

That left Walt and Ken with a furious wildcat in a net that prevented the wildcat from escaping but didn't keep him from getting his claws and teeth into operation.

Ken has a 16 mm. copy of this picture. I have seen it rerun several times and each time Ken lets out a yell at the point the wildcat grabbed Walt's thumb in his teeth and started chewing.

Having to do battle with a netted wildcat on a six-inch trail above a perpendicular drop calls for stamina, agility and the ability to overlook a little thing like a chewed thumb.

The Prowler, headed across the desert.

The boys made it all right. The wildcat was finally lifted off the ground and they started back down the trail. They took a few steps, lost their balance and came tumbling down the ledge to the sandy wash below, wildcat and all. Fortunately at that point the drop was not far enough for them to break any bones.

Another bright idea the producers had was for Walt, while cooking breakast, to pick up a frying pan at the same time he was holding a large bun. It turned out that the frying pan called for both hands, and Walt, thinking to dispose of the bun temporarily, put it in his teeth while he used both hands on the frying pan.

Ken, topping a ridge some distance away and seeing Walt's predicament, was to play a practical joke by loosing a shaft from his bow which would shoot the bun right out of Walt's mouth.

This was all shown in slow-motion pictures.

All in all there were three episodes. At the end of that time the producers had completely run out of ideas, and the strong probabilities were that just about all the people in the audience who saw the pictures thought the whole thing was an elaborate fake.

Walt, who is extremely conscientious, is bothered by this.

"Erle," he said to me, "you know I won't take part in any fake. If I'm supposed to do something, I'll do it. Now, I've been worried a little bit about that match trick. You remember where Ken wants to light a cigarette and takes out a match and I shoot an arrow that hits the head of the match and strikes it?"

I nodded.

"Well now," Walt said, "that shot wasn't entirely the way it seemed. Actually I don't believe you could light a match by hitting the head of the match with an arrow."

"Go on," I told him.

"Well," Walt said, "the way we lit the match was by sticking sandpaper to the arrow. Then we had only to just miss the head of the match with the point of the arrow and let the sandpaper strike the match. Now, I don't like that. That's getting pretty close to faking something as far as I'm concerned."

The skill called for in shooting of this kind is absolutely uncanny. The head of the match must be missed by perhaps a fraction of an inch with the point of the arrow so that the sandpaper, sliding along the head of the match, ignites it.

Walt was also worried about the rattlesnake part of the act, although Ken thought it was all perfectly legitimate. They purposely made the picture on a rather cold morning, and the brothers pointed out that anyone knows a snake is a little sluggish on a cold morning. Although the snake was rattling and preparing to strike, it wasn't anywhere near as dangerous as it would have been a few hours later after it had warmed up in the sun – at least the brothers thought not.

These were the Wilhelm brothers as I first knew them, unbelievably skillful with a bow and arrow and blowgun, wild as the desert winds, filled with the spirit of adventure, and game to try anything.

Later on, Ken designed a car of his own which he called "The Leaping Lena." Walt had The Prowler and Ken, The Leaping Lena, and they continued to go just about every place in the desert.

The motion pictures they had made covered their activities so thoroughly there was nothing new to be added. The great depression came along and had us all in its grip. Ken started operating a desert service station. Walt got a job, and I held my nose to the grindstone until I just about wore a groove in the grindstone.

But we kept in touch with each other off and on through the years and then a few weeks ago Walt wrote me that he

Walt Wilhelm, Louie Roripaugh and Arch Randall starting out to explore the desert thirty years ago.

was going to retire, that he would have a small income and abundant leisure and he intended to get back into the field of adventure.

In the meantime, of course, the development of balloon tires and four-wheel-drive automobiles has changed the picture of desert transportation materially.

Because of my trips into Baja California I am long on four-wheel-drive automobiles, and because I have a warm spot in my heart for the Wilhelm brothers I decided to get in touch with them and see if we couldn't look into some of the odd corners of the desert that only they knew about.

The letter that Walt Wilhelm wrote in answer to mine is so typical that I am going to reproduce a part of it.

Walt writes the way he goes across the desert. He picks the shortest distance between two points and tries to get there without any detours. There is a certain straightforward sincerity about his writing that carries conviction, a between-the-lines punch which captivates the reader.

Here is a part of Walt's letter:

> Well, it's ten twenty five and I just returned from the post office where I got your letter and the Baja book. I'd call you but I'd better write because I'll take plenty time and I won't forget what I want to say.
>
> The first of March is okay with me. I went out to see Ken over the week end and he's all set any time also.
>
> Ken owns the Old Cady Ranch. I could write you many pages on the ranch alone. I went down to the old guard house Sunday just to see if it was still standing.
>
> You perhaps don't want too much of the old ranch, but you couldn't write a book on the desert without having something to say about this old fort. The last soldiers were mustered out in 1882. Here was headquarters for the cavalry. They rode each way on the old trails to protect the Emigrants.
>
> We don't want you to feel as we're guiding you. We just want to take a trip over the old trails just for the hell of it. And it won't take much time to cover what you need for a story.
>
> Now if I could ever catch you when you wasn't in a hell of a hurry. We'd go to Nevada, and along the rim of Death Valley. Where outlaws and bootleggers hung out, and where we had our own weapons ready when we went in there over forty years ago.
>
> Ken found one guy murdered in a cave with his hands chained and they dug up another corpse in a manure pile.
>
> I went with the Sheriff in 1920 to blow up a still where four men had shot it out and all were killed. One guy crawled four miles after being shot four times with a forty-five and died in the arms of an old miner named Rose.
>
> Mr. Rose became a good friend of mine. I used to go over and visit with him. We traveled all over the desert in the early twenties. He mined in Death Valley when they were taking out borax. I've still got a chain he gave me from one of the original borax wagons. This chain is still hanging from a tree in my back yard where it's been for thirty years.

> I was a young man then Erle and I knew many tough characters that was hiding from the law. They didn't bother me and I could always stop at their cabins and get a meal. One old guy at Government Hole drove an old Ford for twelve years and never had a license for his car.
>
> The last stage robber was killed ten miles from my home at Coyote Wells. He held up the Daggett stage and was run down by some miners after he'd crossed the Calico Mountains. I'm quite sure we can get to many places where the average man hasn't been, and possibly no one.
>
> Minerva has been reading some of this letter and says the spelling is lousy and that a sixth grader could do better. Why shouldn't they? I never got as far as the sixth grade.
>
> I'm looking forward to this jaunt with you. It will be the first time in my life that I can go some where and not have to worry about when I get back.
>
> I came out here first in 1916. There's a high peak between here and Barstow that's on the map as Lead Mountain. Well all the old timers call it 17 mountain because there's a natural 17 near the top.
>
> Near Cronise Valley is some hills that's on the map as Cave Mountains. Well, all the desert folks call it Cat Mountain because there is a perfect cat formed with sand on the side and in one big canyon.
>
> I don't know exactly what you're after for a book. I've tried to give you a skeleton of an idea of what's out here. As soon as we get together I'll get your slant and we'll go from there.

I sent a copy of this letter along to J. W. Black who became quite excited about the prospect of desert exploration. He had developed a new type of Pak-Jak and he wanted to test it in sand that would be disastrous to any other vehicle we knew anything about.

This new type of Pak-Jak has to be seen to be believed. Even then, incredulity is likely to get the upper hand.

The tires are huge doughnut affairs, made entirely of plastic, feather-light but reasonably tough. They were designed primarily for sand, but Black wanted to test the

Sammy (Sam Hick's son), Walt Wilhelm and Ken Wilhelm inspect J. W. Black's newest invention for crossing desert sand.

vehicle to see how it would do in sand so soft that it would be impossible to get over it with any other type of vehicle; he then wanted to test it on sharp rocks in order to see how the tires would hold up.

This vehicle was strictly an experimental model.

Along with it, of course, Black had some of his regular heavy-duty Pak-Jaks which would go just about anywhere but which would bog down in climbing certain types of sand hill.

He wrote to ask me if I thought the Wilhelm brothers knew of any place in the desert where there was sand so soft a person would sink almost up to his knees.

I didn't even bother to interrogate the Wilhelm brothers. I wrote Black to come ahead. I told him that the Wilhelm brothers knew the desert and could find anything he wanted anywhere in it.

About this time Bill Berry came to call on Black, saw Walt

J. W. Black shows how the invention works.

Wilhelm's letter and wanted to know if there was a vacancy in the party.

Bill Berry is an expert driver, having been connected with off-the-highway vehicular transportation for years, working with various four-wheel-drive companies, and, more recently, becoming the public relations representative of the American Motor Scooter Association.

We all gathered at my ranch and then drove up to Yermo to talk with Walt.

Ken, it appeared, had taken a long-term lease on the Cady Ranch which contains within its boundaries the old historic Fort Cady and the junction of the Emigrant Trail and the Arrowhead Trail. The place is rich in history and relics.

I found the brothers thirty years older than when I had last adventured with them, and some thirty pounds heavier, and it came as a shock to me to realize that I also was thirty years older and thirty pounds heavier.

Walt Wilhelm, the author and Ken Wilhelm discuss plans for a new trip.

Personally I welcomed the change brought with the passing years. I thought they would be tame enough so a man wouldn't have to jump out from under rolling automobiles or stand perfectly still while they shot an apple off his head.

Ken was always mildly amused at my conservatism. Later on in the trip he confided to Sam Hicks that on his really close stunt shooting he always allowed for a quarter of an inch error so that there was really nothing to worry about. He gave himself that quarter-inch factor of safety.

The Wilhelms got out copies of their old moving pictures and we were fascinated observers of the scene where they lit the match with an arrow, then snuffed ashes off the end of the cigarette which had been lit with the match, and the one where Ken shot a cuff button off Walt's head.

Walt told some stories of the old Prowler trips.

It must be remembered that The Prowler antedated the jeep. When it was manufactured there was nothing like it in existence, nothing that could possibly compare with it.

When Hoover Dam was being put in and the engineers wanted to explore the desert to find the best route for their high power line, which naturally had to go as straight across country as was practical, it was Walt who drove them all over the desert and enabled them to locate the route which the power line now follows.

Walt tossed enough potential adventures into the hopper to keep us busy for months.

For instance, he knew where there was agatized wood, petrified palm and petrified palm roots which the rock hounds had not as yet discovered. He could, he thought, relocate the scene of the old battle between the Indians and the cavalrymen. He knew the site of an old Indian encampment where there were many relics and lots of arrowheads. He knew an old homesteader living in seclusion in a wild part of the desert which he used to explore with his Prowler; and he had the story of one fabulous missing mine which is completely authentic and entirely modern.

A Mexican laborer had been injured and Walt had been instrumental in getting a doctor to him but not in time. The Mexican had died.

When they looked around in his cabin to see if they could find the names of relatives, they found only the most primitive essentials for living: a table, a dilapidated chair, and very little else.

But what interested them was a pair of coveralls, the legs tied at the ankles, completely filled with quartz through which the gold was running literally in ribbons.

Where had this quartz come from?

They searched carefully to see if the Mexican had left a trail from his cabin, but he had been too smart for that.

And of course there was a mystery connected with it. Why would the Mexican have lived in poverty and continued to work for wages if he had such a bonanza at his fingertips? Could he have been planning on making a stake and quietly slipping out of the country for reasons of his own?

Since the man was regularly employed, it was virtually certain that the mine was located within a short distance of his cabin. And since he had been able to amass the ore by utilizing only such spare time as he could command, and only the primitive tools which were found in his cabin, it was evident that the mine was either on the surface or close to the surface.

Nothing much was said about the discovery, but the people who knew about it went back to the cabin and searched the vicinity carefully. They never found the mine.

The ore was fabulously rich, and because of the manner in which the free gold ran through the quartz, it was distinctive enough to have been recognized if it had come from any established mine in the vicinity.

The story of that ore is one of the unsolved mysteries of the desert.

Walt thought we should go out to the place where the man had lived and take a look around. He also felt that if we were going to have a helicopter aiding us in our explorations later on, it would be very much in order to make some low altitude exploration.

While the man was smart enough not to leave a trail from the cabin to the place where he got the gold, it was almost certain that as he approached the location of the mine he must have left something of a trail. From the air, particularly with the aid of a low-flying helicopter, it is almost impossible to conceal any trail. As we noted earlier, tracks that have been made many, many years ago can still be seen from the air.

We wanted particularly to photograph the location of the old Fort Cady. We wanted to follow the Emigrant Trail for some distance. We wanted to use a mine detector in exploring the old campgrounds around the Fort and see what we could discover.

Emigrants coming from the parched desert to the site of the fort were accustomed to rest in its comparative security before heading on toward the Mormon settlement in San Bernardino.

This Cady Ranch is surprisingly beautiful. One comes from the sandy desert down to a ribbon of mesquite, cottonwood and willow trees and is suddenly greeted by the sound of running water. There are a series of small ponds filled with wildfowl, plenty of cool shade and fertile ground.

The adjoining sand hills are literally covered with thickets of close-growing mesquite, so netted together that they are completely impenetrable.

Rabbits live here. There are hundreds of wildcats and many coyotes. Wild ducks dot the placid ponds. The place is a paradise for the water-starved animals living in the desert.

One can well imagine what must have been the feelings of the tired emigrants who reached comparative security, feed and abundant water. They were able to relax with the realization that the dangers of their long arduous trip were behind them. They found unlimited water for bathing and for washing clothes, could watch their livestock eat their fill, and, what was probably as important as anything, found a blacksmith's shop where their wagons could be repaired.

We became so fascinated with the fort and the historical atmosphere that we kept putting off our exploration of the surrounding desert.

With the aid of our mine detector we located the site of the old blacksmith's shop, and excavation brought up old horseshoes, hand-forged nails, springs and other heavy equipment which we were unable to identify.

At Fort Cady, there are ponds, wild fowl and fishing.

We discuss plans outside Ken's new ranch house at Fort Cady.

The old barracks at Fort Cady.

The barracks of the soldiers were still standing; in fact Herman Rodriguez, an Indian about whom we shall presently hear more, was living in one of the small buildings constructed of logs and roofed with mesquite branches covered with earth.

The soldiers, in maintaining law and order, had to make frequent punitive expeditions into the surrounding territory, and occasionally ran into stiff resistance. Sometimes they failed to return.

A huge cottonwood, which until recently had been standing in front of the fort, was known as "The Hangman's Tree" because many an outlaw had come to the end of his career dangling on a rope thrown over its huge branches.

That tree fell within the last few months and is now lying, a huge giant of a dead cottonwood, across the ruins of the fort.

J. W. Black and the Wilhelm brothers had been thinking

Herman Rodriguez, who found the solid gold arrowhead.

All that remains of the old "hanging" tree from which so many rustlers and renegades swung.

along the same lines, how to get over the fine drifting sand of the desert, carrying bedrolls and a reasonable quantity of water and provisions.

The answer as worked out by the Wilhelm brothers was a new type of desert prowler, a super sand buggy, equipped with enormous airplane-type tires that would go over the desert just about anywhere.

We tried it out and found that it was wonderful on the smooth straightaway where the sand was unobstructed but the tires were so large that the leverage of the steering mechanism was inadequate, and on the rougher type of country something needed to be done to the steering mechanism to give it more leverage and power.

Then we tried out J. W. Black's machines.

The conventional Pak-Jak, with its large rear wheel and 6 horsepower air-cooled motor, did a wonderful job going over rough country and very fine powdery sand. But when

The newest Prowler starts out over the sand hills . . .

. . . and comes down a pitch so steep Walt Wilhelm prepares to jump.

The newest Prowler with Ken Wilhelm at the wheel, Bill Berry beside him, Sam Hicks in the back seat.

The author hangs on as The Prowler heads downhill.

Down the hill with the greatest of ease.

we tried out the new machine we were all astonished. Not only did it go smoothly over the softest sand, but it barely left a track. It seemed to float along like a tumbleweed. Moreover, the low air pressure in the light tires absorbed all obstacles and gave the rider a smooth, easy ride.

The Wilhelm brothers certainly got us into soft sand. That was what Black had wanted and that was what he got.

It was so soft that two or three hundred yards of walking in it would wear me out. It was like trying to fight through waist-deep powdery snow. This new desert-going machine of Black's, however, simply glided over the sand and left barely a track behind it.

Black decided to get on back to his factory and put the machine into commercial production.

So then we had the question of what to do and where to go, and there were so many objectives that we hardly knew which one to pick first.

J. W. Black comes up a steep sand hill with the front wheel off the ground, showing the abundance of power. Note that the tracks left in the soft wind-blown sand are hardly noticeable.

Walt Wilhelm, Jean Bethell, the author and Anita Haskell Jones twenty years ago.

For my part I was getting all the thrill I wanted simply renewing old friendships and reminiscing with the Wilhelm brothers. We looked at old pictures, we drove to places where we had had memorable camps in the old days. We watched Walt demonstrate his skill with the blowgun, we looked over his collection of bows and arrows, and endlessly swapped yarns.

Because Ken couldn't join us for a couple of days we decided to investigate the less spectacular projects. We agreed to explore a rock deposit that Walt knew about, which the rock hounds hadn't as yet found, and where there had as yet been no digging.

We got in our four-wheel-drive automobiles and started out.

Walt and I were in the lead. Walt was showing me where to go.

The experience was similar to those I had had with Walt

three decades ago. There weren't any roads to the place we were going and Walt acted as casually as if we were riding across the desert on saddle horses.

"Now, Erle," he said, "there's a deep 'wash' between here and that mountain. We want to get down into it where the banks aren't straight up and down, and then we'll follow the bottom of the wash until we come to a place where we can get out on the other side."

The "wash" turned out to be a veritable canyon, as far as I was concerned. We got down to the bottom, which was filled with drift sand, and fought our way to a dry stream bed where running water had washed away the loose sand. Here we could travel with comparative ease, until we came to a place where we had to churn our way up a steep slope, fighting loose sand in order to get to the top.

But eventually we made it, and then worked our way along to a rock field where the whole surface of the desert was strewn with chunks of petrified palm, some palm root, a lot of agate, and various other rocks that would polish into beautiful objects.

The next day we headed for one of the Indian battlegrounds Walt had told us about. We found an old, old road, long abandoned, the ruts filled with sand.

Walt was pretty sure that this road led to the house of a friend whom he hadn't seen for some twenty-five years, since the days of the old Prowler, in fact.

In those days Walt, who scorned to use roads with his machine, pulled up into the mountains, came through a pass and pushed his way down through sand to the little homestead.

Walt described the place to us as a beautiful homestead, shaded by trees and built in an excavation so that the lower part of the building was buried in sand. He remembered a well some twenty-two feet deep which, though the water

We break a trail to the old homestead only to find it in ruins.

was not the best, nevertheless provided amply for the cottonwoods which in turn furnished shade, and the water was really all right for drinking.

We finally came on the "homestead" and it was pathetic to watch Walt's face; first surprise, then consternation, as he realized something of the toll of passing years.

There was no sign of the occupants. The cottonwood trees were dead. The well had caved in and filled up. The roof had blown off the house, the sides had been ripped loose by desert winds. The excavation in which the house had been built was pretty well filled up with sand.

This was the place where Walt had once stopped and sat under the shade of cottonwoods on firmly packed ground, visiting with a delightful but rather aged couple.

When the attrition of years is seen gradually and in almost imperceptible changes from day to day a man can become accustomed to it, can even become philosophical about it.

J. W. Black has even designed a sidecar for one of his inventions. He gives Ken Wilhelm a never-to-be forgotten ride.

But when the devastating impact of almost thirty years comes at a single blow, the effect is sobering indeed.

Therefore it was in a subdued frame of mind that we left the homestead. After many miles of desert travel, part of which was over a road that was little more than two ancient ruts filled with drifted sand, we came to the site of the first battleground.

The story as Walt heard it was that a marauding band of Indians had murdered a family of emigrants and looted the wagon. Then they had fled into the desert, but the cavalry took up the trail and eventually had tracked them to this place where some of the Indians were killed and some of them captured.

In earlier days Walt had found human bones here and a human skull. He had found many arrowheads, beads and other evidences of an Indian encampment. There was water nearby and apparently the Indians had maintained a secret camp at this little spring.

Now everything was changed. Military tanks had been using the surrounding desert as a practice ground and there were fresh tank tracks and exploded tank gun cartridges. A beautiful Indian metate that had been in the path of one of the tanks was now broken into pieces.

We found some arrowheads, some bones which we thought were those of deer, and some human bones.

Mesquite thickets had grown up around the water and these had evidently been used as practice targets by flame throwers. The tanks must have wheeled into position, directed their flame-throwing mechanisms at the mesquite thickets and turned loose.

In one of these thickets we found a partially incinerated coyote. Evidently the animal had thought it was safe in the deep shade of this thicket as the thundering tanks roared by, then suddenly the thicket was seared by a flamethrower and the coyote was burned alive.

Apparently the military had no idea of the historic significance of the place. There were still plenty of Indian relics lying around, but the depressing effects of the ruined homestead, the bones and partially consumed hide of the dead coyote had robbed us of our enthusiasm.

The brothers told us about another battleground which promised to be much more interesting and exciting. They guaranteed that here we would find no evidences of civilization having tarnished the face of the desert.

Walt had doubts about our four-wheel-drive equipment getting in there.

While this equipment was just about the cream of the crop, it was all conventional without oversized sand tires. We had a Land Rover station wagon, an International pickup, a Ford four-wheel-drive pickup with a camper body, and the Wilhelm brothers had a jeep.

There were no roads where we wanted to go, and we

We go into deep sand in Ken Wilhelm's jeep.

would simply have to take a compass course across the desert. Moreover, the last several miles were up a steady and at times a steep gradient, where we would have to fight loose sand as we climbed.

However, we had power winches on some of our cars which had previously tackled some of the worst sand in the desert of Baja California, although that had been level going, and we hadn't had to fight grades as well.

In any event we determined to try it.

The brothers told us the story of the battle as they had heard about it from old settlers, who in turn had had it from the records of the fort.

A large marauding band of Indians had attacked an emigrant train almost within sight of the fort and then had made their escape.

A detachment of some thirty-five cavalrymen had taken up the trail of the marauders, pressing them closely.

The sand is pretty well chewed up by the various vehicles passing over it.

The Indians had fled up into a box canyon and scampered up an almost perpendicular face of rock of a hundred feet or so.

The cavalrymen had dismounted, climbed the rock face and started in hot pursuit after the Indians.

It is not clear whether the Indians circled or whether the whole maneuver was part of a carefully prepared plan, and a detachment of Indians had been left behind, concealed in the boulders of the canyon.

What *is* certain is that either the cavalrymen had not left a guard with the horses or if they had left a guard, the guard had been overpowered. The Indians stole the horses of the cavalrymen and drove them away, leaving the cavalrymen on foot far from reserve supplies of ammunition and in the midst of a dry, parched desert.

Apparently there were no survivors. The full story will

We kept to the sand-filled washes until they became too narrow to follow.

never be known. Such records as were available came from the lips of victorious Indians who boasted from time to time about what had happened, and in the mute evidence which a rescuing expedition found on the ground.

Walt and Ken had found parts of saddles and quite a few human bones at the scene of the battle which had stretched out over the desert for several miles.

I understand that one other prospector found some brass buttons.

Since we had our mine detector with us, we had high hopes of unearthing something, but we reckoned without the problems of transportation.

We started out moving easily across the desert, then came to the first slope and its dry drifting sand.

We kept working our way up a terrain which became steeper and steeper as we climbed, our destination a scar in the side of a mountain which was plainly visible.

We lose the uphill fight with deep sand and have to use a winch to get out.

As the washes narrowed, they became filled with drift sand. We had to fight our way, leaving behind us a network of tracks as each driver would try to pick the best route and avoid places where the car ahead had "churned" the soft sand.

The problem was how to get the cars up the steep banks to the rougher but more open country on the sloping plateau.

What with one thing and another, it was late in the afternoon when we reached a rock-filled canyon which forced us to leave the automobiles and go ahead on foot.

There had been a terrific windstorm a few days before, one of those desert sandstorms which sometimes disclose objects that have lain buried for years, or sometimes through the vagaries of the wind, bring in fresh quantities of sand and cover everything.

We found to our dismay that the windstorm had blanketed the entire area we wanted to explore.

Herman Rodriguez tells the author about finding the gold arrowhead.

This loose, freshly drifted sand also accounted for many of the difficulties we had encountered with our equipment and had slowed us down so that we were about two hours behind our schedule.

However, we looked around over the scene of the battle for an hour, took some pictures, and then reluctantly started back toward the Mojave River. Sometime when a wind from another direction has swept away some of this sand, or after a desert cloudburst I will return to this place. Walt is going to keep his eye on the weather and phone me when there is an advantageous time for another go at it.

Next time I hope J. W. Black will have enough of his new sand-conquering machines so we can all ride up rapidly in comparative comfort.

There was no difficulty following our tracks on the way

back. We had left plenty of them, and since we were going downhill now, we returned to camp in short order, arriving about dark.

It was at camp that we unearthed an interesting story. From Herman Rodriguez, who has been working at the Cady Ranch for years, we learned of the arrowheads he had discovered. He brought out several different types to show us, then he mentioned the solid gold arrowhead.

At first we thought this was simply one of those stories one hears from time to time in the desert, but after checking carefully we came to the conclusion that the gold arrowhead actually exists.

Herman had found it at the site of an old Indian encampment and had submitted it to an acid test to determine that it was really gold. He had of course kept it as one of his prized possessions.

Later his mother became sick. When the doctor visited her he saw the gold arrowhead and became intrigued by it. He offered to settle his entire bill then and there for the arrowhead, and Herman took him up on it.

Others had seen this gold arrowhead, and Ken Wilhelm, while he had never seen it himself, had talked with one thoroughly reputable person who had seen it and vouched for Herman's story.

Considering this story in connection with the story of the Mexican laborer whose coveralls were filled with gold ore, it becomes apparent that there are infinitely rich mines in this part of the desert which have not as yet been rediscovered.

Under the influence of the balmy sunlight, the clear, cloudless sky, the soothing effect of our surroundings, we became as indolent as the old covered-wagon emigrants who had entered the tranquil atmosphere of this desert oasis and had succumbed to its beauty.

The Desert Is Yours

We just couldn't bring ourselves to stick to our program of exploration.

We had, for instance, intended to follow the Emigrant Trail for miles in the Pak-Jaks, using a mine detector to see if we could pick up bits of metal.

We put this program into execution but followed the Emigrant Trail for only a few hundred yards. We found several old-time cartridge cases and a well-worn piece of metal which came from an old singletree. Then after exploring some sand hills nearby, we decided to return to camp for lunch.

We never went back.

Walt Wilhelm standing on the old Emigrant Trail . . .

. . . where the depressions and wheel ruts are still visible.

There was some discussion about the fact that this would be a separate expedition in itself and there was no use splitting up the trip.

At this point the Emigrant Trail was easy to follow. The ruts had been filled in and sections of the trail had been completely covered by thick mesquite growth, but the passing of many hundreds of covered wagons had left an indentation in the desert which could easily be followed.

Some day we intend to go back with Pak-Jaks and follow that trail across country.

We found that exploring the old Emigrant Trail in the vicinity of Fort Cady with a mine detector gave us altogether too much exercise.

We had expected to hear only an occasional "beep" from the mine detector, but the instrument was almost continu-

Bits of iron and an old cartridge, relics of the Emigrant Trail, are corroded with the rust of ages.

ously giving forth its distinctive sounds indicating the location of metal.

Sometimes our digging would uncover an old tin can which had undoubtedly been left years ago by some careless camper, but for the most part the bits of metal we found were exceedingly interesting; old horseshoes flaked deeply with rust, bits of hardware evidently dropped from the covered wagons, and of course empty cartridge cases.

Some of these cartridge cases, while undoubtedly very old, were difficult to date because they fitted guns manufactured both in pioneer times and long after the days of the covered wagon. We wondered about the stories these cartridge cases could tell.

It is almost certain that these expended cartridge cases

would have been saved for reloading if they hadn't been fired during some urgent circumstance. Perhaps the bullet had been directed toward a hostile Indian, perhaps toward a deer which was only wounded and had to be dispatched.

We will never know.

We learned of one man who had picked up an old powder horn which I would have liked to have photographed, and some day I expect to go back and get a picture of it and also to try and trace the solid gold arrowhead.

We were here at a time when the eastern part of the United States was shivering in temperatures which at times reached well below zero. Yet we were basking in the warm sunshine, inhaling the clear, dry air, and relaxing under the desert's influence.

The Wilhelm brothers' lunch and picnic retreat is enclosed on three sides, the fourth open to a sun-swept reach of riverbank.

The Wilhelms had erected a three-sided roofless structure on Ken's ranch, containing a long table, benches, stove, sink and other conveniences, including some overstuffed chairs and a couch.

The fourth and open side was within some fifteen feet of the water and less than fifty feet away there was splendid bass fishing.

The open side of this building was on the south. The three closed sides were on the east, north and west, and with warm sunlight pouring in we would eat lunch and settle back in the comfort of a couch and overstuffed chairs or stretch out on a cot.

When Walt and I settled down here, the result was perfectly disastrous as far as any fixed schedule of activities was concerned, and we let the others do the exploring.

There is, however, one nice thing about approaching the desert in this way. It means that we are going back in the near future. We have left a wealth of material for subsequent trips.

We want to follow the old Emigrant Trail. We want to look for the mine from which the Mexican laborer took rock that was literally riddled with gold ribbons. We want to get back to the scene of the battle between the Indians and the cavalry after a windstorm has blown sand away instead of bringing it in. And we have dozens of other plans.

But after all, those lazy hours when we sat and drowsily watched the wild fowl swimming over the placid surface of the water, when we built air castles and talked over adventures we had shared; all were characteristic of the charm of the desert – winter-warmth and sunlight, the feeling of tranquility, the absence of stress, the pure atmosphere; all a part of what the desert has to offer.

Chapter Nine
Pinky, Helicopters and Lost Mines

There were three objectives on our list of explorations: The Lost Dutchman Mine, The Lost Arch Mine, and The Lost Dutch Oven Mine.

All three would necessitate helicopters to evaluate certain clues we had as to their location, respectively in the Superstition Mountains, the Turtle Mountains, and the Clipper Mountains.

Once I had sat down and figured out the amount of time the helicopters would be available versus the number of things we had to do with them, it speedily became apparent that we were going to have to sacrifice some of our objectives. The question was, which ones?

We had some tantalizing clues to the location of the Lost Dutchman Mine in the Superstition Mountains to the north and east of Phoenix.

This mine had apparently been discovered many times. At one time it was possible to locate it readily and to take out a small fortune within a matter of a few days. The trouble was that it was deep in hostile Indian territory and the people who went into that territory were almost invariably killed, or simply vanished into thin air.

However, Sims Ely, in his book entitled, *The Lost Dutchman Mine,* published by William Morrow & Company in 1953, discloses the result of many years of search and careful study. There are enough clues in that book for one to stand a very good chance of locating the mine by the use of helicopters, despite the fact that the Indians spent all one winter carefully concealing it.

There has never been anything quite like the Lost Dutchman Mine and the trail of tragedy which has followed in its wake.

There is no point in trying to retell the entire story of the Lost Dutchman Mine because there simply isn't room and it is too complicated a story. Sims Ely's book runs nearly two hundred pages and is packed full of facts. It would be worse than useless to try to condense those facts into the brief space available here.

Suffice it to say that in the early days a Mexican family discovered the mine and took out a fortune on several trips, always having a sufficient force to discourage Indian attacks.

Then the Indians gathered in force. The Mexicans, a whole pack train laden with gold, were starting out of the mountains.

The Indians made a surprise attack, killed most of the Mexicans, cut loose the packs, leaving the gold scattered on the ground, led off the livestock and later killed and ate the horses.

Since that time numerous lucky finders have found caches of gold where it had been cut loose from the pack horses, and Jacob Waltz, the "Dutchman" of history, evidently found the mine itself.

We gave the situation careful study. Sam Hicks did a

tremendous job of research and marshaled all the clues he could get into an outline supported by a detailed map. We might even find the pot of gold at the end of the rainbow. But in any event we would have fun using the helicopters.

Our plan was to establish a base camp at the Superstition Montains and afterwards move in with the helicopters.

Sam Hicks, J. W. Black, Jack Hicks, and David Hurtado took some of my four-wheel-drive vehicles, a lot of camping equipment, and drove to Phoenix, then on into the Superstition Mountains.

The Superstition Mountains have to be seen to be believed. In fact, even seeing them doesn't immediately bring about belief. One feels like the farmer who went to the circus for the first time, saw a giraffe and, after a brief survey, expectorated tobacco juice profusely and delivered himself of his final judgment, "There ain't no such animal."

The boom which has come to Arizona is incredible. People have discovered the warm, sunny winter climate, the health-giving dryness of the crystal-clear atmosphere; water has been brought in and has transformed the desert into an area of fertility, and luxury resorts have sprung up like mushrooms. The result has been a phenomenal growth which is far more than a boom — it is an explosion.

Phoenix, in turn, has become a vast sprawling metropolis, and where once there were outskirts, desert and unmarked roads, we now have freeways, traffic congestion, suburbs, and a sea of houses.

Then suddenly the Superstition Mountains rise up as a veritable wall to turn back the tide of civilization. Within a distance of perhaps a mile and a half or two miles we go from a thriving metropolis to a land that is as wild and rugged as the human mind can imagine, a land where greed and naked passions levy a continuing toll; a land where persons who leave the main trail should be armed and alert.

A cursory glance at the history of this country, with its stories of violence and death, will convince anyone that searching for the Lost Dutchman Mine is a rare experience in itself.

An interesting sidelight on the story of the Lost Dutchman Mine is that it is probably the only lost mine which has been underwritten by what amounts to a chamber of commerce.

Some of the leading merchants in Phoenix and vicinity have banded together in an organization known as "The Dons," and this organization has not only kept alive the legend of the Lost Dutchman Mine, but has even acquired a camping site at the beginning of the trail leading into the lost mine territory.

Within certain limitations people are welcome to use this camping site on expeditions which are actually sponsored by The Dons, and once a year they make a big ceremony out of a mass search for the Lost Dutchman Mine.

Soft drinks and hot dog stands are opened up at the camping grounds. Busses bring people out by the hundreds. Everyone joins in the excitement of searching for a mine which is probably hidden within a few miles of the camping place, and which may well be found on one of these expeditions.

The Hiller Company was sending two helicopters, one from the factory, one from a point northeast of Phoenix. Pinky Brier was going to fly me over to join the ground crew and be there when the helicopters arrived.

Then a whole series of unforeseen events took place. A terrific storm struck Northern California, blowing down trees, closing roads, sending rain in torrents.

Sam Hicks telephoned me from Arizona, much disturbed. After his arrival, he had been told that the area in the Superstition Mountains had been declared a wilderness area and it was illegal to use any mechanized equipment of any sort.

Not only would it be impossible for us to use Pak-Jaks in exploring the country, but we couldn't even land a helicopter there.

This last was a fatal blow.

We had certain sections mapped out, which we wanted to explore by helicopter. We felt that if we could hover over these places at a low elevation we could find some significant clues – but it would do us little good to find clues and then be unable to land to investigate.

We could, of course, mark the area and return subsequently on foot or by horseback to make our investigation, but our whole plan of operations had been to use these helicopters on a continuous basis, moving from one point to another.

Rather reluctantly I temporarily moved the Lost Dutchman Mine from the head to the foot of the list, and told Sam to break camp and return to Amboy in California where there was a good landing field and where we could make a rendezvous with Pinky.

In the meantime I decided to join the caravan and explore available camping sites as we moved on from Blythe to Amboy via Needles.

I met the ground party on schedule at Blythe and we went up to Needles, made camp to the south of Needles, then moved on into the Old Woman Mountains and went to Sunflower Springs.

It will be remembered that Sunflower Springs was the place where the two prospectors, Packer and Kohler, were to join forces and where Kohler was to start out for the Turtle Mountains to show his partner the natural arch he had discovered.

The Old Woman Mountain range is a massive backbone of sheer granite sloping down to the sandy desert, marked by a huge peak of granite which looks for all the world like a

The pan and iron pipe keep up a continuous clanging in the desert wind.

Tom Farley, left, his dog and the author.

sculptured old woman sitting up on the very crest of the ridge, looking out over the sun-swept desert.

At Sunflower Springs we met a man named Tom Farley, who was living alone in a cabin, and liking it, his sole company a dog and a cat.

On occasion Farley made trips to town for supplies. However, a trip to town involved a long journey over dirt roads which consumed gasoline and tires, and while Farley was rich in leisure, we gathered he was not particularly affluent in worldly goods.

Farley had some tame chukkars that he fed, and a couple of burros. He was at the moment out of baking powder and the bread he was trying to make without baking powder was a pretty soggy concoction.

We noticed that he had a griddlecake cooker tied to a tree, and nearby was a piece of iron pipe. Whenever the wind blew, the pipe and the pan beat together in a monotonous clanging.

We asked Farley about it and he explained to us that that was to keep him from talking to himself too much. When there was sound he didn't have to talk, but when there wasn't anything to keep his ears occupied he used his own voice.

The logic of this was not exactly apparent but it was reasonable enough to Farley so we accepted his explanation at face value.

A few miles below Sunflower Springs we made a dry camp. Then the next day we decided to go into Essex for supplies and asked Farley if he wanted a ride.

Farley did.

The little store was also the post office.

Farley hadn't been in for some time. There was one letter for him which he opened in our presence and out of which he took two one-dollar bills.

The interior of Farley's cabin.

He hesitated for a while, then took the two one-dollar bills, which we suspect represented his sole available cash capital, over to to the grocery department and bought two dollars' worth of dry dog feed for his dog.

The next day we met Pinky at Amboy. Then Pinky and I started out to locate the helicopters, knowing only that they were to make a rendezvous at Las Vegas and then get in touch with us at Sunflower Springs.

We felt we could save half a day of helicopter flying time if we could pick them up.

Joe Templeton happened to have been at my ranch the night before I started out to join the group at Blythe. I told Joe, "You got me started looking for this Lost Arch Mine thirty-five years ago and now you're darned well going to have to help me find it."

Joe was ready, willing and eager, as they say in the law-books, so when we met Pinky at Amboy, where she arrived exactly on schedule; we climbed into her twin-motored plane. I suggested that she fly in the general direction of Las Vegas and get on the radio to see if we could pick up any clue as to the location of the helicopters. Since the plane would travel much faster than the helicopters we felt there might be time to make a quick circle around the Turtle Mountains while we were using the radio.

Pinky is a stickler for having the latest and the best in radio equipment on any plane that she takes off the ground, and she is equally careful about filing flight plans and keeping in touch with various checking points as she puts her plan into operation.

Recently I had heard a couple of interesting stories about Pinky. I asked her about them while we were flying along and got at least a partial verification.

A few weeks ago Pinky was flying back from Las Vegas late at night.

A prominent citizen who had gone for a drive into the desert with his family, including young children, had failed to return, and there was considerable apprehension on the part of people who knew his plans.

The desert is a picturesque playground and yet it can turn almost instantaneously into a cruel death trap.

Along toward midnight word was flashed to the authorities and there was talk of searching parties the next day.

Searching the desert, however, is quite a job. There are many, many square miles and compared with the immensity of the area a car is rather a small object.

Then somebody thought of Pinky, who was flying back from Las Vegas.

It was a black night and the chances of finding a stranded party in the desert at night were just about nil, but Pinky is used to accomplishing miracles.

Pinky knows the desert like most people know their back

The Devil's Playground.

yard. She wanted to know when the party had left, and in general where they planned to go.

Then she did some fast thinking.

If the party were in that general area, there was a particularly dangerous death trap known as "The Devil's Playground." Not only would the party be likely to want to explore it, or at least take a good look at it, but the fact the car had not returned meant it was some place where it couldn't get back, either because of a mechanical failure or because of being trapped in sand. In the latter case there was the strong probability that the wheels had dug down into the sand.

Pinky listened to the information on the radio, said, "Okay, I'll take a quick look."

She was already past that area of the desert but, always willing to oblige, Pinky turned the plane back toward Las Vegas. Due to her remarkable sense of direction and her knowledge of the desert, even in the dark night she was able to fly over the desert until she came to The Devil's Playground.

She made a couple of circles before she saw the fire—a little pathetic pinpoint of red flickering down in the desert.

Pinky banked the plane, circled down until she was skimming the ground, and by the light of the campfire saw the frightened faces of the cold children, the man gathering firewood, the car bogged down in deep treacherous sand.

Pinky made another pass to let them know she saw and understood and then got on the radio, giving such accurate directions that within a short time a rescue party had picked up the group and sped them to hot food and warm beds.

The other story concerned a flyer who started from Las Vegas for Long Beach and ran into clouds. Trying to fly up above them, he got to around fourteen thousand feet, had no oxygen and not only became disoriented, but disoriented to such an extent that when the tracking stations finally picked him up in response to his call for help and told him where he was and what to do next, he simply couldn't believe them.

What this man didn't realize was that not only was he in great danger because of fuel shortage and disorientation, but that the clouds had developed icing conditions and his plane could be wrecked by ice.

This time the tracking stations again thought of Pinky, looked up her flight plan and discovered she was again flying the night skies, this time on her way from Los Angeles to Palm Springs with some passengers she had picked up at the International Airport.

Pinky was asked by radio if she could go "upstairs" and rescue a man who was in a lot more danger than he realized.

Pinky put it up to her passengers, who regarded the whole thing as a lark, so Pinky headed "upstairs."

The ordinary flyer would have iced up and wrecked long

before reaching the fourteen-thousand-foot level where it was relatively clear and where the plane with a disoriented pilot was cruising on a course that was rapidly getting him nowhere except into trouble.

The radar at March Field guided Pinky, and her flying sense guided her around the clouds, where she followed the warmer updrafts which exist before the atmosphere socks in solid.

Finally a relieved radar operator said, "Okay, Pinky, he's all yours. He's about one mile dead ahead at twelve o'clock at your elevation."

Pinky came up on the plane's wing, tuned in on his wave length and gave him instructions to follow.

Two or three times the man who had been flying at high elevation with no oxygen questioned Pinky's ability and drifted off course.

At those times, Pinky, who was well aware of the danger and knew the necessity for perfect teamwork, proceeded to tell him a few things in an unladylike language which brought grins of appreciation to the hard-bitten flyers anxiously listening in on radio and watching on radar.

Pinky twisted and turned her way down through the dark corridors of the sky, avoiding icing up, and got the man directly over the field just as his last drop of gas squeezed out of the tank.

Pinky takes all this in her stride.

So now, flying over the desert we kept Pinky busy on the radio while we took pictures and worked out an itinerary for the helicopters—if we ever located them.

We felt that they probably were either in Las Vegas or just getting to Las Vegas, so Pinky contacted the airport there but drew a blank.

Realizing that we had an hour or so to spare before we could expect to contact the helicopters at Las Vegas, I suggested to Pinky that we might take a swing around the Turtle Mountains.

I had previously explored the Turtle Mountains in a somewhat desultory manner, looking for the arch which Kohler found and which presumably was the location of the famous Lost Arch Mine.

The maps show that there is a road leading to a spring or a well at the north end of the Turtle Mountains. It is called Carson's Well and presumably was named after Kit Carson or one of his descendants. I decided that this would be the last place to look for an arch, because if an arch had been in that vicinity, it would certainly have been discovered years ago. I had directed my search toward the more central and eastern part of the Turtle range, despite the fact that reason told me whatever Kohler had discovered must have been toward the northerly end of the range, and that the arch which marked the location of the famous Lost Arch Mine must almost certainly be located at the north part of the range and on the east slope.

Since so many people had used the road to Carson's Well to get into the Turtle range, I had avoided that part of the mountain.

Now, with Pinky at the controls of the twin-motored plane we decided to make a complete circle around the entire range.

This exploration certainly wouldn't be as effective as the one we could make by helicopter, but it would give us a general idea of the lay of the land, show where we wanted to start our explorations and make our camp, and there was always the possibility that we could turn up an arch.

Pinky made an almost complete circle of the Turtle range without finding anything and then we flew over the part of the mountain that is just beyond the extension of the road.

It was Joe Templeton who saw it first.

Our first exciting view of the arch we discovered in the Turtle Mountains.

"An arch!" he shouted. "An arch!"

We looked where he was pointing and sure enough, there was a natural arch—a beautiful natural arch, halfway up the side of the mountain.

We asked Pinky to put the plane in a tight circle so we could make a survey of the arch and I hurriedly snapped pictures of it.

There could be no doubt that this was a natural arch which had been there for many thousands of years, and was undoubtedly the arch that Kohler had seen. It did not, however, match the general description of the arch beneath which Fish had filled his pockets with gold.

Then suddenly I realized that *no one had ever said there was any similarity between the two arches.*

The similarity was one of those things that had been taken for granted.

Fish had reported finding gold in the shadow of an arch which was in the Old Woman Mountains. Then years later

Kohler had simply mentioned that he had found a natural arch in the Turtle range, and because Kohler had never heard of the Lost Arch Mine and Packer didn't want to arouse his suspicions, there had never been any verbal comparison of the two arches.

We were almost certain that this was the arch Kohler had discovered and had described so many years ago to Packer.

The interesting thing was that of all the people who must have seen this arch in the Turtle Mountains during the last ten or fifteen years, apparently no one had ever thought to connect it with the arch described by Kohler; in fact, we found that very few people knew anything at all about the Lost Arch Mine, including many of the old prospectors I had spoken with recently.

We were in a high state of excitement as we told Pinky to start flying north and to contact the airport at Las Vegas.

Pinky tried and finally got through to the airport by radio relay, but drew a blank. The helicopters had not been there.

Pinky contacted other points, searching for two helicopters and then, as she changed wave lengths on her radio, suddenly listened in on a fragment of a conversation which she thought was between helicopter pilots.

She listened some more and sure enough, found out she was right.

Pinky cut in, made herself known, explained that I was in the plane with her, and asked where the helicopters were.

It turned out they were in Searchlight, Nevada.

Because we had had so much trouble contacting them, I told Pinky to tell the helicopters to wait right where they were and we'd fly up to join them.

Pinky's twin-motored airplane, with a speed of two hundred miles an hour, made short work of the distance. We flew to the north over the desert, crossed into Nevada, came down at Searchlight, and found the helicopters waiting.

One of the helicopters flies over the arch.

Naturally we all wanted to start out right away. We wanted to get back to the arch in the Turtle Mountains. We wanted to do about fifteen different things, all at the same time.

Bob Boughton broke the news to us. The helicopters were packed to the last ounce of lifting capacity. They couldn't take on passengers. They had camp equipment, sleeping bags, personal baggage, cameras—all sorts of equipment. They were loaded.

Pinky came to the rescue.

"Load all the stuff in my airplane," she said. "I'll fly it to Amboy where the four-wheel-drive vehicles are waiting, and load it into the cars. Then I'll pick up a load of passengers and come back to join you. In the meantime you can take my passengers in the helicopters once the load has been transferred."

That was a practical solution and we started shifting loads.

The capacity of Pinky's airplane was absolutely amazing. She turned it into a cargo plane carrying heaven knows how much weight.

In the meantime we climbed in the helicopters and started for Needles where we landed and had lunch, then went on to the Turtle Mountains. We made a detailed survey, hovering over the arch, circling the surrounding terrain looking for a suitable camp site, and trying to locate a place reasonably near the arch where we could set a helicopter down.

Unfortunately there wasn't a place near the arch which we could use as a landing field, even for a helicopter. The ground was sharply sloping and by that time considerable turbulence had developed.

Meanwhile Pinky had gone to Amboy, transferred her load, given instructions to the drivers to join us at a camping spot which we would pick out by helicopter, and then had returned to keep in communication with the helicopters by radio.

Despite the fact the desert is likely to be warm in the winter (although there are very definite exceptions during periods of north wind when it can become bitterly cold) it is still subject to the equinoxes and afternoons are just as short in winter as those elsewhere in the same latitude.

Almost before we realized it, the sun had dipped behind the Old Woman Mountains and we were out looking for the pickups.

We located them, led them into a good camping spot, the helicopters set down and then the trucks came in and the fellows set up camp.

We had quite a camp that night. It had been a day to celebrate, and there was a lot to discuss.

It soon became apparent that for every hour flying time at our disposal we had plans that called for from five to six hours time. It was a question of what to eliminate.

I have encountered this same problem before with an editorial request for three thousand words on an important subject. I start out first getting the ideas I want on paper, then to my consternation find they have run eight thousand words. Then I get the article cut down to the bare bone, only to find that it is still running five thousand words. Somewhere along the line I have to take out two thousand words. Every such word that I edit out represents heartbreak.

It was the same way with this expedition to the desert.

However, we finally worked out a scheme by which we would alternate personnel between helicopters and motor vehicles. We would take turns exploring and we would at least cover the Old Woman Mountains to see if another arch which answered the description we wanted could be picked up there.

We all agreed that the arch found by Kohler was in all probability the one we had located, yet was not the arch Fish had found.

The next morning it was my turn to be driving cars. Some of the others were to explore the Old Woman range and then join us along the road.

We started our equipment rolling north right after breakfast and the helicopters took off to explore the Old Woman Mountains.

It was a thrill to see them going about the exploration in a businesslike way. One of them would hover for a while near a curious formation in a perpendicular wall, then dart like a hummingbird for two or three thousand feet, only to pause and hover, then rise up a thousand feet, move over a quarter of a mile, hover; drop two thousand feet, start up a canyon to the end, rise for an over-all look at the scenery, then drop down to follow the next canyon.

And of course all the time the pilots were communicating with each other by radio.

Sam Hicks and J. W. Black, on Pak-Jaks, and Jack Hicks on a Burrito start out for the arch in the background, which is farther away than it seems.

One of the helicopters takes off.

We made better time that day than we had expected with the rolling equipment, so when it was my turn to ride in the helicopters, we were all the way back to the highway with the vehicles.

Reports on the Old Woman Mountains were discouraging. There was a lot of territory to be explored—too much for us to be absolutely certain the helicopters hadn't overlooked an arch. But they had, for the most part, covered the entire range, flying up the canyons and making a survey.

One of the helicopters had found a place where it looked very much as if an arch had been destroyed by an earthquake. A pile of rubble in a canyon gave every indication that such an arch had collapsed; but here again the ground was too sloping for a helicopter to land and we had to appraise the situation while flying back and forth.

This place, however, was definitely one worth looking into.

We crossed over into the Turtle Mountains to see if there were any chance that the arch we had found might be only one of two or more arches.

It was my turn to be in the helicopter at this time and I got a great thrill out of hovering alongside the perpendicular ledges, stopping to look into caves, rising to the summit and drifting down to the lower levels, skimming the floors of the canyons.

We found several arches, some of them merely holes in the rocky ledges, none of which exactly fitted the description of the arch that had started all the excitement some eighty years ago.

We marked several places for ground exploration, landed several times and scrambled up steep slopes looking at interesting outcroppings. And again the day moved on as though the sun had been following a greased track across the heavens.

We went back to the highway, picked up the rolling equip-

Using a walkie-talkie, Jack Hicks explores one of the arches.

Looking through the arch down the face of the mountain.

ment and moved down to our next objective, the Clipper Mountains, where we made camp that night.

It will be remembered that it was in the Clippers that Schoefield found the famous Lost Dutch Oven Mine.

We compared notes on our various helicopter trips and found that we had so many places marked to investigate further by means of automobile and Pak-Jak that we would be busy pretty much all winter.

Pinky, being restricted to the larger landing fields at Amboy, Needles, etc., had gone on back, leaving the helicopters to pick out suitable camp sites and signal us in.

It had been quite an expedition, and despite our weariness when we gathered around the campfire everyone wanted to talk at once. We had so much to tell, had seen so many things and had had so many experiences, that it was as hard to cover the territory by means of a verbal report as it had been to cover the terrain by helicopter and crowd everything in that we wanted done.

These interesting apertures in the rock formation are not true arches, they are holes bored by sand-bearing wind.

Chapter Ten
The Lost Dutch Oven Mine

When the Santa Fe Railroad was constructed it literally fought its way across the desert, and the fight had necessitated huge supplies of water. Hauling water in was so expensive the railroad decided it might be possible to dig a tunnel in the Clipper Mountains to the north of the little station of Danby and bring water some twelve miles to the railroad through a pipeline.

In those days this was a tremendous undertaking. Earth had to be moved laboriously with a "Fresno" scraper and mules. Both men and mules had to be provided with water.

Schoefield was employed by the railroad. On one of his days off he explored in the Clipper Mountains and what he found has become history—the abandoned mining camp with its big Dutch oven filled with gold.

Schoefield was never able to retrace his steps. He remembered certain landmarks, but the excitement of his discovery, the distance he had covered, coupled with the fact that a cloudburst had wiped out his tracks and washed out many of the landmarks, prevented him from ever returning to his discovery.

In later years, when telling friends about his adventure, he stated that he had followed a wide trail and had come to two portals so close together a loaded pack burro could squeeze between them only with considerable difficulty.

Nowadays when the Santa Fe's crack passenger trains, The Chief and The Super Chief, glide over a smooth roadbed, it is difficult for the passengers sitting inside in air-conditioned comfort, eating, drinking, reading, playing cards, to imagine the time, effort and money which made all this possible.

We are inclined to look upon the "investment" in terms of today's operations. A tunnel and a twelve-mile pipeline—why, *that's* nothing! Tractors and earth movers would take care of it easily. Let the railroads have a fair return on their "investment" but let's regulate their freight rates, etc., etc., etc.

The Santa Fe Railroad's crack trains speed luxuriously through country where prospectors once risked their lives.

The helicopter bringing Pak-Jaks in to the Clipper Range for an exploratory trip.

What we lose sight of is the fact that the dollar of today is not the dollar of seventy-five years ago and that the investment of time, human effort and downright sweat, plus the problem of pioneering a railroad through a hostile country was an undertaking of such magnitude that it can't be measured in today's dollars and cents. It must be measured in terms of man hours, in terms of dripping perspiration, in terms of human courage, human labor, and human danger.

I wrote the Santa Fe Railroad to find out something about the location of the tunnel, the date of its construction and about Schoefield.

The railroad was most accommodating. It sent me a wealth of material, so that we at least knew where to start our search, and by examining the various records we picked up certain clues that were highly significant.

The Clipper range of mountains is relatively smaller than the others we had explored and since this was the last loca-

Two views of narrow portals in the Clipper Mountains.

tion on our list of objectives, we had made a base camp and unloaded our Pak-Jaks, expecting to leave the cars right where they were.

This meant that we could explore by helicopter and if we found anything interesting in suitable terrain, the helicopters could get the Pak-Jaks, bring them in and ferry personnel back and forth, so that everyone could get in on the search.

It wasn't long after we started the next morning that the people in one of the helicopters reported they had found the portals through which Schoefield had passed—or at least had found narrow portals which answered the description.

This caused quite a bit of excitement. We made a rendezvous at this place, sent one of the helicopters back for Pak-Jaks and started exploring with the other helicopter.

Now, it must be remembered that what Schoefield found was more than a mine. It was an abandoned tent with a huge

Dutch oven, and this Dutch oven in turn was filled with gold. Schoefield had brought back proof of his story by filling his pockets with this gold, which we understand subsequently returned him more than a thousand dollars.

After the Pak-Jaks came in and we started really covering the territory, we began to unearth some rather significant clues.

I found the lid of a teapot, an old rust-encrusted lid of obsolete vintage, buried in the sand. There were other indications of a very old camp.

We also found many things leading us to believe we were pretty close to the spot Schoefield had described.

Using the helicopters it had been easy. The trouble was it had been too easy.

We had a feeling that others had been there ahead of us.

If one discovers a lost mine, he is likely to specify the location of the mine and then make an announcement to the effect that he has found the mine; but if one uncovers a huge Dutch oven full of gold, what then?

Theoretically the person rings up the Bureau of Internal Revenue and says, "I have just discovered a fortune in gold in a Dutch oven. Please send your form X-Y-Z number 20467-J for me to fill out."

This is theory.

We have a strong suspicion that in practice it might not happen that way.

Nevertheless, here we were to the best of our belief standing very close to the spot where Schoefield had found the abandoned tent and the Dutch oven filled with gold.

According to the story which Schoefield told his friends after recognizing his inability to retrace his steps, he had passed through the narrow portals and followed the trail for a distance until he came to the remnants of a tent. This tent was a semipermanent structure, having been erected upon a

The helicopter prepares to move our camp.

wooden frame, but the canvas had rotted and was blowing in tatters.

Inside, there were the remnants of provisions, a table, plates, and every indication that men had left the place on an absence which was intended to be temporary—perhaps merely a sojourn to the mine which they were working.

After exploring the country and finding a mine which had very rich ore, Schoefield had returned to the tent and then had investigated the Dutch oven, finding it full of gold.

Reconnoitering by helicopter from the air, the finding of topographical clues is rather simple, and in fact one gets a general knowledge of the topography which would be difficult to acquire in any other way.

Even so, it was some time before we found what we felt to be the actual location of the tent, and this was bolstered by the fact that in digging we actually came upon remnants of rotted canvas and bits of wood which had evidently been part of an ancient tent stretched upon a wooden frame.

The Desert Is Yours

But the most exciting discovery was when our mine detector began to beep, and digging disclosed what could only have been the handle of a large-sized Dutch oven.

Yet continued search in the territory failed to disclose any other trace of the Dutch oven, so we used the helicopters to move our gear back to the main camp.

It is our opinion that the Dutch oven, with its contents of gold, has been discovered and removed.

Certainly whoever discovered such a fortune would have no reason to disclose it. There might be claimants to the estate of the dead mining partners on the one hand, and there most certainly would be the inexorable grasp of the government on the other.

However, as I have mentioned previously, we wouldn't know what to do with a lost mine if we found it. The pleasure is in the hunting.

The helicopter picks up a bundle of tents, sleeping bags and cooking provisions.

Chapter Eleven
A New Slant on the Famous Lost Dutchman

The time had come to bid farewell to the helicopters. We stood and reluctantly watched them ascending from the canyon, skirting the ridges, winging their way over the summit, then gaining elevation into the blue desert sky and finally heading north until they passed from sight.

While conditions prevented us from profitably using helicopters in the search for the Lost Dutchman Mine, we decided to take a quick look at the country by airplane, and so Pinky was once more called upon.

In many ways this was one of the most remarkable trips I have ever taken.

We flew over the desert, exploring from the air various and sundry places to which I want to return—places where there are clues which point to lost mines, to romantic adventure, and unusual surroundings. Then we glided in to Yuma for lunch, and that afternoon moved out over Arizona, skirting Phoenix, landing at Mesa, and then being driven to one of the modern motels at Apache Junction.

The distinctive "Weaver's Needle" dominates the Superstition Mountains. The Lost Dutchman Mine is supposed to be almost within the shadow of this peak.

Anyone who has not searched for the Lost Dutchman Mine has missed a thrill.

In our case the search was made by air, but most often it is made by foot.

Aside from the physical effort and time expended there is little difference in the potential thrill.

One leaves urbanization behind and in the twinkling of an eye finds himself in surroundings so primitive that the days of the old Wild West are forcefully brought to mind. Nor is the danger entirely fanciful.

One needs only to consult the files of the local newspapers to realize that human life is held very cheaply in the Superstitions.

On the main trail, and in numbers, people are presumably as safe as on the sidewalks of Phoenix; but wander off the main trail to explore, making overnight camps in the Superstition Mountains and . . . well, before you start, drop into the newspaper office and read some of the accounts of the more recent killings.

A New Slant on the Famous Lost Dutchman

Sam had made the acquaintance of William R. (Tobey) Drummond, a cowpuncher and horse trader who had been raised in the country and knew much of its traditions. Drummond told us off the record about some of the killings that had taken place.

He had not only been a deputy sheriff but he had actually been a member of the posse that had gone in the Superstitions to arrest some of the men thought to be responsible for the killings.

His stories were remarkable but the man's integrity was vouched for and he told them with sincerity.

He also had souvenirs: the rifle of one of the men who had been accused of killing in a feud which had flared up over a spring, and he told of having to arrest a Westerner who was chain lightning on the draw.

Even now, Drummond shakes his head when he mentions it. That man could get his gun out and fire it so fast that the human eye could scarcely follow the motion.

"Why," Drummond said, "my son has practiced and has

The Superstitions are incredibly rough.

Drummond displays the gun of a killer who was acquitted by a jury on the ground he had acted in self-defense.

become much better than I ever was with a gun. He can hold his hand extended in front of him with the palm down, a fifty-cent piece on the back of his hand. He can turn his hand until the fifty-cent piece slides off and then before that fifty-cent piece reaches the floor he will have drawn his gun and fired accurately into a man-sized target."

"This desperado in the Superstitions could beat that?" I asked.

"He was not exactly a desperado," Drummond said cautiously. "He had had a criminal record. He was wanted for questioning and it was my job to help with the arrest. I was one of three persons sent in to pick him up. In the end we had to trick him in order to get the drop on him. I have never in my life seen anything as deadly fast as that man with a gun."

Then Drummond went on to tell us a story he believed to be true but which he personally couldn't vouch for. It came to him from a friend who, he felt, was thoroughly reliable, an old Indian who lived on a reservation and who had little use for the government which treated him as a child.

While prowling through the Superstition Mountains, this Indian had come on a dry wash which had recently been flooded by one of the flash floods that sweep through the desert country in the summer.

This flood had exposed an underground hoard in which there were several bars of gold.

The Indian had carefully concealed all but one of these bars of gold. That remaining bar he had taken to the reservation to see if it would be possible for him to dispose of it in a legitimate manner.

He was taken before the authorities, questioned at length and then questioned again. Their attitude was hostile and suspicious. They demanded to know exactly where he had found the gold.

The Indian told them. He told them in great detail everything that they asked for, except that the place he described so graphically was far removed from the place where he had actually found the gold.

The authorities took the gold from him for "investigation." He never heard any more about it: he never got the gold back.

And so the Indian has said to hell with it, if he couldn't keep the gold he wasn't going to tell the white man where it was.

The story may or may not be apocryphal. Our friend believes it.

Sitting in his cozy, modernized log cabin, listening to him tell the stories of the Superstitions with some hesitancy because he didn't want to be accused of exaggeration, listening

A hard core of lava is all that remains of this extinct volcano.

to the care with which he commented on the things he could vouch for and the things which came to him secondhand, I was tremendously impressed.

One thing is certain. If there is a bit of the West that remains really wild and untamed and yet within a few short miles of urban life, it is the Lost Dutchman Mine and the Superstition Mountains.

A man can stay in an air-conditioned motel, surrounded by every luxury, and the next morning, after a short automobile ride, find himself in a country where he is treading ground that has been baptized by the blood of still-fresh Western feuds, or move along a trail that passes within a mile or two of one of the most famous and most fabulously rich lost mines of the West.

Then, after a long hike back, he can plunge into a steaming hot shower, return to the bar, and with his appetite sharpened by exploration and exercise enjoy some of the finest food available anywhere.

It is incongruous that this should be so. Yet it is so.

And if the man wants to arrange with some of the packers and outfitters who are available to carry saddle horses to the foot of the trail on trailers, he can take a two-day trip which will cover every nook and corner of the mountains accessible by trail.

As our airplane survey showed, however, there are all sorts of rugged terrain in which there are no trails. It would be possible to conceal a thousand Lost Dutchman Mines in the Superstition Mountains.

But one should heed the advice printed on the menu of the restaurant in the motel. If one goes into the Superstition Mountains to camp overnight, he should not go alone; he should be accompanied by others and all should be armed.

The hard center cores resist erosion.

Chapter Twelve
Three Hundred Stunt Cars in the Desert

The City of Indio, Queen of the Coachella Valley, site of the annual date festival in California, is strongly influenced by the surrounding desert.

Palm Springs, La Quinta, and the valley to the west have absorbed most of the retirement and resort business, and Indio has been left as a business island in the midst of the desert.

A few years ago Indio was hot during the summer, balmy and beautiful in the winter, but hardly the place one would pick for year-round living if one was primarily interested in comfort and relaxation.

Now everything is air-conditioned, and of course the air-conditioning business itself has become quite an industry.

My friend, Bill Bryan, is the past president of the local "Jeep" club, The Sareea Al Jamel 4 Wheel Drive Club, and because I wanted to cover an annual four-wheel-drive excursion into the desert I entered into correspondence with him about their next annual "drive," and as time for the drive drew near, Sam Hicks and I went down to talk over details. The name, Sareea Al Jamel, incidentally, means "fast camels" and was chosen primarily because Indio is the site of the annual date festival, but also because the name is in keeping with the theme of the festival.

I had asked to have Sam go along in the lead car and cover it from the ground and I intended to arrange with Pinky Brier to cover it from the air.

I had never before become involved in any of the various club activities. Business commitments necessitate that I curb my natural impulse toward gregariousness.

When an author wants to do a little adventuring on his own, when he has a weekly television show, when he has writing commitments evidenced by ironclad contracts with publishers, and a thousand other interests—each clamoring for attention; when mail comes pouring in an avalanche each day, there is little time for forming new friendships.

I well remember when I first came in contact with people who had become famous in the writing and motion picture world and noticed the ruthlessness with which they protected their privacy. I determined that if I ever became successful I would never change, but would always have ample time for "visiting" with people who wanted to see me.

How little I realized the problem.

As I became more successful, more and more people wanted to visit with me, both in person and by mail. Whenever I tried to be friendly, those casual contacts invariably led to more contacts; readers who had written me and received a cordial reply to their letters came to see me; people who had been entertained on a brief visit came back for longer visits, then told friends about it and were importuned by those friends to be permitted to meet the author. I soon realized that if a man didn't do something to protect his privacy once he got in the public eye, he would literally be trampled to death.

For this reason I have of late avoided making contacts with

clubs, associations and groups where such contacts bid fair to complicate my problems.

More recently I have come to realize this is a mistake. One shouldn't shun public contacts. Most people are considerate, extremely so, and once the problem is explained to those who aren't entirely considerate one finds them willing to cooperate.

I mention all this merely to explain why my desert expeditions so far had been made either alone or in the company of only a few intimate friends.

However, the four-wheel-drive clubs have become too important to be ignored. I wanted to see one of them at first hand, and from what I knew of the Indio club I was satisfied it offered one of the best opportunities to see what was going on. Moreover, we were already friendly with Bill Bryan.

Bill gave us a cordial invitation to come along on the trip, so Sam Hicks and I drove over to Indio to have a preliminary chat with Bill and his fellow member, Cliff Gentry, who had done so much in mapping out the course of the "drive."

It may be mentioned parenthetically that Cliff drove all along the route of this expedition as troubleshooter, and his driving, his ability to handle a crowd of people, to know what needed to be done and get it done, aroused Sam's wholehearted admiration—and Sam is a hard man to impress in such matters.

Bill Bryan is in the refrigerating business and one becomes immediately aware of what has been happening in the desert in the last few years by walking into Bill's place of business.

In the foreground is a big machine which automatically manufactures ice cubes in quantity. There are large-sized paper drinking cups and the temptation is irresistible to slide back the glass door, fill a paper cup with ice cubes, turn on the nearby tap and drink the cool water while chatting.

It happens that Cliff, in addition to being Bill Bryan's principal business competitor, is one of his closest friends, and quite a bit of good-natured chaff went on at luncheon.

That luncheon itself is indicative of the changes that have been taking place in the desert.

Instead of going into a hot room, humid with the perspiration of other diners, redolent of the smells of cooking inescapably entrapped within the walls, we entered a hotel dining room that was pleasantly darkened, perfectly ventilated, cool and comfortable, despite the fact that the thermometer outside was well up in the nineties.

I have been raised in a school which holds that any business lucheon should be over by one-thirty, but in this dining room the seats were comfortable, the service was good, there was an excellent bar, the food was fine, and no one seemed to be in a hurry.

I was shocked to find it was after two o'clock when I called for the check and made a belated apology to my guests.

Bill laughed. "Think nothing of it," he said. "We do this all the time. After all, I have my principal competitor here with me."

Somehow I have an idea this statement wasn't just a courteous rejoinder to my apology. The desert seems to have cast its spell over the tempo of business life in Indio as well as the manner in which the people live their lives. They are happy, healthy, and they enjoy their work as well as their play.

All the people at lunch that day were four-wheel-drive enthusiasts.

That meant that they ran their businesses on weekdays, and on Saturday afternoon and Sunday climbed in their four-wheel-drive vehicles and went places and did things.

The local club had about twenty-three cars, which isn't a gauge of membership because a woman who is married to

The kids eat it up.

a four-wheel-drive enthusiast pretty often develops a liking for the sport and winds up being just as enthusiastic as her husband. And the kids literally eat it up.

I thought I knew a little something about four-wheel-drive vehicles and about how to handle them. I knew, of course, that I was a safe, sane, conservative driver. I had made trips down the entire length of the Baja California peninsula on several occasions when we had literally made our own roads, or used our vehicles to follow some goat trail or go up some sandy wash where we were the first wheeled vehicle ever to enter the country.

As it turns out, I am the rankest sort of amateur—although I didn't find that out until later. When these people talk of four-wheel-drive excursions they are talking about post-graduate work as a point of departure.

There are all sorts of vehicles in these four-wheel-drive clubs: the conventional jeep; the souped-up jeep; the Land Rover, which is the English version of four-wheel-drive mechanism; the International Scout; the souped-up Volkswagen; the Japanese versions of four-wheel-drive, the Datsun and the Toyota, and the four-wheel-drive Ford pickups.

Many of the cars have extra powerful motors installed. The jeep will perhaps have a V-8 or a six cylinder motor from a car like a Chevrolet, but it may have an overdrive as well. Then two wheels will be cut in such a way that when the parts are again welded together the space between the rims has been very much widened so that oversize tires can be mounted, thereby giving added traction, particularly in sand. There is simply no limit to what human ingenuity and mechanical ability can accomplish with these things, and, as I soon learned, there is almost no limit to what these machines can do.

It is one thing to follow a rough, steep road leading from one place to another, or to explore a sandy wash, working out a pass through the mountains down into the other side; and it is quite another thing to deliberately seek out ridges and hogbacks where the slightest miscue can lead to disaster.

Cliff Gentry, as the latest member to roll his car over and over, has to put the club emblem on his car upside down, and will keep it this way until some other unfortunate member makes a miscalculation; then the new member will take over with the upside-down emblem and Cliff can put his own back right side up.

When Cliff earned the upside-down emblem he really did it the hard way. Apparently his car rolled over five times before reaching a stopping place.

The real veteran four-wheel-drive enthusiast takes this in his stride. His car is equipped with roll bars on top, with seat belts, and either has a winch to pull out with, or some other member of the expedition will be certain to have a power winch.

However, at the time we joined up with Bill I knew very

Cliff Gentry. The upside-down emblem on the car indicates his was the most recent roll-over in the club.

little about their operation. I was interested in four-wheel-drive exploration of the desert country, and while I knew that these clubs had regular excursions over courses which simply took off across country, I had little idea what they were like.

Bill Bryan seemed to be addicted to understatement.

"There was a time," he said, "when we used to make these courses pretty rough. Only the really experienced four-wheel-drive experts could tag along. We separated the men from the boys. Then we eased up. We started making them just exciting enough so they'd be interesting. In that way we got a lot more attendance. Members of the family began to come, wives and kids, and everyone had a good time. So now our courses aren't really very difficult."

What an understatement that was. And what a sport this four-wheel-drive exploration is!

As I said before, there was a lot of good-natured banter between Cliff and Bill.

Bill, it seems, was driving a souped-up jeep with a V-8 motor, an overdrive, heavy-duty winch, etc., which had originally been owned by Cliff.

As Bill explained it to me, the car was so speedy and smooth-riding with all of the stuff Cliff had put in it, that when they went out together on weekends Bill's wife wanted to ride in Cliff's car — it was faster, smoother-riding and more comfortable. Bill explained that he had been forced to buy the car in order to get his wife back.

Cliff was now driving a souped-up Volkswagen with big tires and a special motor. Bill, with the restlessness of all persons who are addicted to some fad, was looking around for something new, and announced that he was thinking of selling his car after the run on Saturday and Sunday; so I began inquiring about price and wanted to know whether I could count on Bill's wife riding with me if I bought the car. This brought an emphatic negative from Bill, despite my status as a senior citizen well past retirement age.

Up a steep slope.

Whoa there! You're starting to skid.

Bill's club has twenty-three cars and I had assumed that the run would be more or less of a small, intimate family affair with a few outside clubs sending representatives.

Actually, up to date over two hundred cars had registered for the drive, and some four hundred and fifty tickets for the barbecue had been sold.

As it turned out, there were about 322 cars which finally registered to participate in the drive — with a total attendance of 978 people, 478 of whom were served at a deluxe barbecue by Vance Young, a professional who specializes in catering to this type of outdoor gathering. His last party had numbered over two thousand.

Until one gets beneath the surface and realizes what is happening on these drives, he has absolutely no idea of the fascination of this form of amusement. It is comparable in every way to outboard-motor boating and may well prove to be as fast-growing and as popular.

One of the priceless remarks of the luncheon was con-

Coming down one of the steep grades, this guest rider decided he would rather walk.

tributed by Bill, who goes all out for the things he likes. He wasn't trying to be funny but was simply describing someone. Bill said with enthusiasm, "He's my kind of people. He's a nut."

Naturally I was becoming more and more interested in this new sport I was investigating. We completed arrangements for me to cover the run from the air with Pinky, while Sam Hicks would take a camera and ride with Cliff Gentry.

I met Pinky promptly at eight o'clock at the Palm Springs Airport and we took off for the scene of the drive, making a few detours first in order to check over some of the desert country I wanted to see.

I had become interested in the line of the San Andreas fault, with its long succession of palm trees in the valleys, long straight rows of palms, sometimes in single file, sometimes where water is in evidence, in clusters.

At our luncheon I has asked Bill about them and about getting in there with a four-wheel-drive vehicle.

"Sure, you can get in there," he said.

"It looked beautiful from the air," I told him. "There were many clumps of trees with deep shade. I should think you folks would go in there often."

He shook his head. "Those places are for the litterbugs. We don't want to get mixed up with them. They leave trash around, scatter beer cans all over the place and leave dirty camps.

"You take any driver who belongs to a club and he's well disciplined. He wouldn't think of throwing out a beer can. If he did he would have to pay a fine. We leave clean camps."

I had this in mind as we flew toward the place where the four-wheel-drive caravan was being camped that night.

Bringing approximately a thousand people into a camp in the desert, particularly when a large number of them have to arrive around midnight, presents something of a problem,

Part of the "city" that came into being overnight.

and I felt if the club could keep control of a situation of that sort it would be almost phenomenal.

I had told Bill that Pinky and I would show up around eight-thirty and take some photographs of the camp and of the automobiles from the air. Then we would fly over to an old abandoned government airport some four or five miles away and he could drive over and pick us up and we'd come down and visit for a while.

We made our first pass over camp promptly at eight-thirty and established contact with Bill through a citizens' band walkie-talkie.

He told us that things were running according to schedule and that the leaders had started out right on time.

Cars were still coming along the highway and pouring in to the camp, and a long line of four-wheel-drive vehicles was just getting well strung out on the run.

Pinky and I made a pass over the cars, then flew on to

take a look at the run and for the first time I began to realize something of what these runs mean.

Here were some three hundred cars strung out in a long single file. Figuring an average distance between cars of fifty feet, that meant a string of cars around three miles long, and that's quite a string of cars.

Already the terrain was beginning to get rough; hills so steep that it seemed impossible any wheeled vehicle could get up them, then coming down into dry washes, following sandy barrancas for a way, then up steep banks, into the foothills of the desert mountains which the vehicles proposed to cross.

We made several passes over the string of cars and looking ahead I began to have my doubts whether those who had laid out the course of the drive hadn't been altogether too optimistic.

We went back and circled the camp and by walkie-talkie I arranged a rendezvous with Bill at the airfield.

We made a landing and Bill and his wife, Carol, came driving up within a matter of minutes. We piled in Bill's souped-up jeep and headed back for camp.

This was quite a camp. Many of the car owners had rigged up little trailers which could be carried on behind over rough roads. These varied from the little camping trailers consisting of a covered double bed, to ammunition-carrying government surplus trailers which had been fixed up with all sorts of fancy gadgets.

On the road they made compact units which would go just about anywhere the car would go, within reason, of course. However, looking over that drive ahead I knew there were places which simply didn't come within the realm of reason.

We met quite a few of the people at the camp who had decided to rest and relax in the desert sunlight, rather than

The camera flattens out the grades, but the sides are so steep that the jeep, off the road, rolled over the sidehill. Sam and Cliff, standing by the jeep, wait for the rest of the drive to get by so they can get the car back in circulation by winch and man power.

go on the drive. We looked around camp and I realized that Bill hadn't been just talking in what he had to say about rules and regulations.

There were trash containers and all of the trash, cans, loose papers, etc., were in these containers. I didn't find so much as a piece of paper drifting around on the desert, despite the fact that a tent-and-trailer camp the size of a small city had sprung up overnight.

After a visit we went back to the airport and then, with Bill and Carol with us, made another survey of the drive.

By this time the leaders had got into some really difficult terrain. Cars were going up a hill so steep that it simply didn't seem possible for any mechanism on wheels to get up it. Then there were steep downgrades on the other side, and finally the drive came to the "point of no return."

This was a very hazardous stretch along a hogback, perhaps a mile or so in all. It is a very narrow hogback, dropping

Point of no return.

down, climbing up two or three times, then finally on the other side, terminating in a downgrade so steep that it was absolutely impossible for any vehicle to get back up under its own power. There simply wouldn't be traction for wheels. The grade was so steep that it was a veritable shoot-the-chutes. Moreover, it had to be taken with all four wheels in a straight line. If a car once started skidding to one side or the other it would roll over and over.

Here and there some of the drivers were having trouble, but for the most part cars occupied by a gleeful driver, wife, and perhaps one or two small children, were negotiating a trail which even from the air simply scared me to death.

This ridge was justly named "the point of no return." Once an automobile got out there there was no way for it to get back. It was on a hog-back so narrow that it was impossible to turn around, and only the most skillful driver could have backed up for more than a few yards. Then the road terminated in a straight-up-and-down line.

Pinky piloted the plane around the line of cars in a series of figure eights, while I snapped pictures and communicated with Sam Hicks by walkie-talkie.

Then we went back to the airport. Bill and Carol got in their souped-up jeep and went back, and Pinky and I made another pass over the line of cars.

By this time quite a crowd had gathered in one place. One of the cars had gone off the hogback and had rolled over four or five times before it had come to a stop. Fortunately the car was equipped with roll bars and the driver was strapped in the seat and sustained only superficial injuries. It seemed that he had encountered a bottleneck, had had to stop his motor, and then when he was ready to go on, in order to try and start the motor had kicked the clutch out as he pressed the starting button. The brakes wouldn't hold on such a steep slope, the car had gained momentum and gone over.

Righting a rolled-over car.

That was the only serious mishap of the entire trip, and after the caravan had passed and the drive had been completed, Sam and Cliff went back, righted the jeep, winched it up and drove it to camp.

This sport looks a lot more dangerous than it really is, but to say that it is thrilling is an understatement.

Later on, after Sam and I had joined forces in Palm Springs, he told me of covering some of the steep grades, watching the cars bouncing and jumping over obstructions, their wheels spinning, a grinning driver at the wheel, a happy wife beside him, and a couple of kids in the rear seat jumping up and down in ecstasy.

Apparently these families had had so much experience with four-wheel-drive vehicles they had lost all sense of fear and were enjoying the thrill to the limit.

From the air, the survey I made was impressive, not only from a viewpoint of seeing miles of cars stretched out over the indescribably rugged desert terrain, but of the economic factors involved.

Tricky driving.

Here were some three hundred-odd cars. (I think the official figures showed 316 cars actually participated in the drive.) There were quite a few cars which stayed around the camp and didn't go on the drive, but even under conservative estimate there was somewhere between half and three-quarters of a million dollars invested in equipment alone.

I made no attempt to count the number of tents and trailers in the camp, but that also represented a goodly investment.

These people are getting a great deal of enjoyment from the arid desert, and at the same time making a contribution to the economy of the country.

The last car, driven by a veteran driver, stopped to pick

On its nose.

up beer cans which had been thrown out and that night around the campfire Bill put it right on the line.

"Some of you folks have ignored our rules," he said. "We picked up quite a few beer cans from the desert. We know some of the people who did it, some of them we don't know. I have just this to say to you people who threw out beer cans. Don't come back next year. We don't want you."

The next day the Indio club members were out policing the drive, picking up odds and ends and cleaning up the grounds. They didn't bury this stuff but took it all the way out to the county dump.

For two weeks thereafter, the members of the club put in weekends going over the run, making sure that they had picked up every can and every scrap of paper. They left the desert just as they had found it except for the tracks made by some three hundred-odd vehicles over places which the average person would have said were utterly inaccessible to any wheeled vehicle.

This Indio club is only one of scores of similar clubs, most of which act as hosts once a year to the other clubs.

It takes the Indio club a full year to police the old runs and lay out new ones so there is a different route each year. And the members have fun doing it.

Around the desert there are literally dozens of club-hosted drives during the course of the year, and hundreds of people get healthful enjoyment from them.

One of the better known four-wheel drive expeditions into the desert is the annual rediscovery of the Anza Trail.

Juan Bautista de Anza, the Spanish explorer, and founder of San Francisco, worked his way through from the parched Colorado desert to the coast by following an obscure Indian trail.

For many years the exact location of this trail was unknown. Then a very remarkable man, Herbert Eugene

Bolton, decided to try and trace the route taken by Anza. Since the explorer had left a rather complete diary, and since from time to time there were references to physical landmarks in this diary, Bolton thought it might be possible to retrace Anza's footsteps if he could find someone sufficiently familiar with the country.

In the course of his investigations Bolton stumbled upon Fred Clark, a salty, rawhide character who lived alone out in the desert and knew every inch of it.

Bolton took a translation of Anza's diary and sat down with Clark.

Thanks to a mutual friend, Louie Roripaugh, who was a protegé of Fred Clark's, I met him during his last years and talked with him about the rediscovery of the Anza Trail.

Fred Clark was a peculiar chap with several well-defined idiosyncrasies of speech. Whenever he meant "yes" he would say, "why no."

"Why no, Gardner," he said, "there wasn't anything to it. At least, getting a start. When Bolton read me certain passages from Anza's diary, I said, 'Why no, Mr. Bolton, that camp isn't over five miles from right here,' and then I took him out and showed him the camp."

Once they had established certain key camps it was not too great a task to follow Anza's trail foot by foot, and Bolton did a wonderful job of research, adding greatly to the history of California.

Some twelve or fourteen years ago when the four-wheel-drive vehicles began to make their appearance in numbers, someone conceived the idea of following Bolton's description and going back on the old Anza Trail.

This annual expedition has now become a ritual and is participated in by hundreds of motorists.

The desert is timeless, yet the desert is constantly being changed by time.

Chapter Thirteen
The Flowering Desert

The desert is, of course, a land of little rainfall. Otherwise, it would not be a desert.

Much of the time rains come during the summer months in the form of cloudbursts which bring flash floods.

The most important thing to remember about camping in the desert, particularly during the summer months, is that one should never, never camp in a dry stream bed. Not only have many people lost their lives by so doing, but many persons who have escaped with their lives have lost their sleeping bags, their camping equipment, their provisions, and at times, their automobiles as well.

A person will be sleeping soundly in the pure desert air, the stars will be unwinking in blazing brilliance, yet up in the foothills or in the mountains a few miles away a sudden black cloud may form and, without warning, explode into a cloudburst which becomes a wall of turbulent, roaring water racing down the canyon as abruptly as though a dam had broken.

The camper may or may not hear the sullen roar of water descending.

It may be that he will waken early enough to be aware of his danger, be able to jump out of his sleeping bag, grab his shoes, which after all are about the most necessary articles of wearing apparel in the desert, and race for high ground, getting there just as the wall of water comes tearing into camp, inundating everything.

If he is less fortunate, he may be sleeping peacefully only to find himself rolling end over end, trapped in his sleeping bag, buffeted by a flood of water from which it is difficult to escape.

There is another type of desert rainfall, however, and this is the occasional seasonal rain in the desert.

For the most part, California, Arizona and New Mexico enjoy dry seasons and wet seasons.

In Southern California all the rainfall, or virtually all of it, comes in the winter (excepting those flash floods in the desert). Usually high mountain walls trap the rain clouds and rob them of their moisture before they can reach the desert, but occasionally, if the clouds are high enough and the disturbance is deep enough, the clouds will coast over the mountain ranges and drench the desert with a gentle rain which will soak the surface of the sandy soil. This water sinks deep enough to germinate the seeds of the desert wild flowers.

Shortly afterward, with the coming of warm weather, the desert will burst into bloom.

No one can appreciate desert wild flowers until he has seen them, or at least seen colored photographic slides.

It seems impossible that so grim and forbidding a place as the desert could become such a garden of soft flowers, such a sea of color.

It is, of course, not every year that this happens; but every

A huge verde tree.

two or three years it does happen. Then the desert becomes a veritable flower garden with verbenas, poppies, lupins and dozens of other species forming a carpet so thick that in places it is impossible to see the sandy surface of the desert below. One can see only a riot of color.

At such times the high mountains which usually throw the

desert into a "rain shadow" will be snow covered, and since these mountains are in some cases as high as two miles above sea level the white snow on the crests will last until early summer.

It is an inspiring sight to see the desert carpeted with a profusion of wild flowers, backed by purple mountains, which in turn are topped with the pure white of snow against a deep blue sky.

When the desert blooms, even its thorny, forbidding shrubs burst into brilliant blossoms.

One of these, the ocotillo, always reminds me of the breadsticks one encounters in an Italian restaurant, only it has thorns all over it and seems to grow without any regard for symmetry or beauty. Yet after one of the desert rains the tips of its arms will unfold into great, vivid red flowers which, outlined against the deep blue of the desert sky, make an unforgettable sight.

One who has never seen the desert in its festive garb should make a point of getting out in it during the wild-flower season. Once he has seen it, he will join the thousands who make annual pilgrimages to the desert at wild-flower time.

Nature has few displays of beauty in abundance which can match the desert during the time of the spring wild flowers.

To be sure, this season lasts only for a comparatively short time, and later on when one sees this same section of the desert parched and bare, dancing with mirages or shimmering heat waves, it is hard to imagine that a few weeks earlier this same ground which now appears to be nothing but dry sand was a flower garden vivid with reds, lavender-blues, yellows and whites all mingled together in a kaleidoscope of beauty.

This is merely another paradox of the wonderful, baffling, forbidding, exciting wonderland we call the desert.

Chapter Fourteen
Getting Gold Out of the Desert

The desert is now coming into its own. It offers health-giving recreation, adventure, excitement, a chance to get away from it all, and the boon of vast acres of public land which are adjacent to paved highways and within a few miles of teeming cities.

Yet the background of its history is filled with tragedy. Mines have been discovered, mines have been lost, and mines without number have been abandoned.

It is surprising the number of mining camps that have been abandoned in the desert. Each one of them represents blasted hopes and unfortunately a decrease in the store of our natural wealth.

My father, who was a mining man, had an idea for subsidizing gold mining which certainly seemed logical.

He pointed out that only a fraction of gold mined was used for monetary purposes. Most of the gold went into jewelry, ornaments, tooth fillings, etc.

My father's idea was to put a tax on gold that was used commercially and in jewelry and from this tax subsidize the production of gold.

This would take a little doing from the legalistic standpoint but it would have a tremendous influence on the economy of the country.

There are lots of abandoned gold mines on the desert. There are many hundreds of these mines that could pay their way if it weren't for the fact that the price of gold remains constant while the price of everything else goes up and up and up and up and up and up.

As a result a man who opens a mine today must have employer's liability insurance, must pay Social Security, must pay high wages, must furnish proper living conditions for labor, must pay high costs of transportation to get his ore to the mill, and then has to sell his gold at a price that is fixed by the government and which is completely disproportionate to inflated costs which go into producing that gold.

Yet the country needs gold, and the country has gold lying in the ground in large quantities ready to be poured into the gold reserves and strengthen the economic structure of the country.

The reason this gold is not put into circulation for the benefit of the community is that no one has as yet devised a scheme that would make it economically possible for the miner to lift the gold out of the ground.

This is a tragedy, for the miner, for the community and for the country.

These abandoned mines represent grim monuments to economic inefficiency.

And, more poignant than the economic question, is the question of human tragedy, the wasted years, the dissipated capital, the heartbreaks.

In one deserted mining camp in the desert I found a

Tragedy is suggested by this homemade toy abandoned at a deserted mining camp.

Christmas or birthday toy probably made by a father for his son. It was a truck that had been laboriously and ingeniously constructed of bits of scrap wood — a present any boy could be proud of.

The mining camp was deserted, the truck was lying there on a sandpile, apparently where the boy had finished playing with it.

What had happened?

Had the boy become ill, and in that isolated desert camp, far from any medical or hospital aid, had the illness proved fatal? Or had the mine, feeling the economic pinch of higher and higher costs of operation and lower yield, been forced to close down and the family working it move out under such adverse conditions they could take only the bare necessities with them?

I don't know, but that abandoned present of the wooden truck spells a story of heartbreak no matter how one looks at it. Normally the boy would have taken it with him as one of his most prized possessions.

It seems incredible that our economists and our lawmakers have not devised some scheme by which mining can be restored to the status it occupied when gold was first discovered.

Once that happens, people will throng into the desert by the thousands, the older mines will be reopened, new rich discoveries will be made, and a stream of golden wealth will pour into the government coffers, strengthening our gold reserves and our national economy.

The facts of life being what they are, this probably can't be done simply by increasing the price of gold. It will have to be done by giving the miner some sort of a bonus. But once this is done, the effect on the nation's economy will be startling, doubly so in the Western communities surrounding the desert.

The desert is still dangerous, cruel, and kind; it still has its health-giving properties and magic. And the man who has been trained in its ways has acquired wisdom, poise and health.

As the pressures of population intrude upon the desert, it is, so to speak, opening its arms to humanity.

The desert is no longer a wasteland to be ignored. It is a place for fun, recreation, and health-giving hobbies. The four-wheel-drive automobiles, the scooter, and big balloon tires; air conditioning, human ingenuity and the constantly increasing desire to get out beyond the smoggy confines of urbanization, are all having a terrific effect.

More and more, people are coming to love the desert, to understand it, to appreciate it, and to enjoy its crystal-clear atmosphere.

This is *your* desert.

Get out in it and enjoy it.